HISPANIC FURNITURE

FRONTISPIECE

VARGUEÑO (S74)
Early XVII century.
Walnut. Interior of
cabinet, visible here, is
brilliantly gilded, as are
the iron mounts on the
drop front (shown in Fig.
129). This *vargueño,*
described in text on page
139, is in the collection of
the Hispanic Society of
America, New York. The
accession number is listed
in parentheses above.

HISPANIC FURNITURE

From the
Fifteenth through
the Eighteenth Century

SECOND EDITION, REVISED AND ENLARGED

by

GRACE HARDENDORFF BURR

THE ARCHIVE PRESS

NEW YORK   1964

Published by The Archive Press, Inc., New York

Library of Congress Catalog Card Number 64-22364

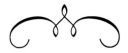

FOREWORD

THE first edition of *Hispanic Furniture* appeared in 1941. Only a thousand copies were printed, and they quickly found their way onto the reference shelves of libraries, museums, collectors and designers. Despite a steady demand, the book has long remained out of print, and has now become almost impossible to find.

With the present edition the book returns to print in a much larger format. The author has revised the text, enlarged the list of references, and added many new illustrations, many of which have never been published.

Her book has become even more timely than it was a generation ago, when American decorators used to put Spanish furniture into picturesque tea rooms, amid a coy masquerade of patched plaster. Nowadays, after a depression and a war have simplified our way of living, our plainer rooms have become worthier of the rugged nobility of Spanish walnut planks, and the sober gesture of their wrought iron fittings.

Spanish cabinetmakers largely ignored the European tradition because they catered to special conditions. The simplicity of Moorish interiors survived in Spanish quarters rather like some of ours today, where bright cushions on a conversation platform created a circle of warmth and intimacy among austere white walls. Spanish courtiers, moving about even more than we, needed tables that knocked apart for stowing on mule carts, and filing desks (*vargueños*) that locked like wooden trunks, with supporting trestles that unscrewed into three pieces.

Once this furniture is set up and in use, no child's obstinate little boots can dent it, and no martini glass can blanch a ring. Its blend of handsomeness and practicality offers lessons for today's designers.

A. HYATT MAYOR
President,
Hispanic Society
of America

PREFACE

I wrote the first edition of *Hispanic Furniture* during the six years that I was Curator of Furniture at the Hispanic Society of America. The book is based on research in the archives and collections of the Society, visits to private and public collections in this country, and study trips to Europe. For information about the craft of woodworking in old Spain I sifted through the wealth of medieval and renaissance manuscripts, incunabula and early books at the Society, and for details about domestic life I studied old Spanish novels, paintings, guild records and inventories of household goods. The book contains a number of illustrations from these sources depicting the furniture and interiors of the period.

In the present edition, as in the first, I have emphasized the furniture of the sixteenth and seventeenth centuries, that great period when the cabinetmakers of Spain and Portugal developed the strong and original style that distinguishes their work from the furniture of the rest of Europe. Also, I have purposely stressed domestic rather than church furniture, which belongs more properly to the province of sculpture. Thus the book is somewhat selective, despite my intention to offer the reader a representative survey of the subject in both text and illustrations. The present edition, with its revised text, numerous additional photographs (many of them never published), and improved format will give the reader a broader view than the first edition.

Many of the new photographs in this edition depict pieces in American collections; they were chosen not only to demonstrate the quality and quantity of Spanish cabinetwork to be found in this country, but also because American collections now house much of the antique Spanish furniture still in existence. Many fine examples came from Spanish collections that were sold here during the first three decades of this century. This wholesale export of antique pieces, which the Spanish government curtailed by law in the late 1920's, has proved in the long view to be something less than a misfortune for Spain. Ten years later, hundreds of great houses and their furnishings were destroyed in the Spanish Civil War, leaving to Americans the responsibility for preserving part of the national heritage of Spain. In a way this book, too, will help to preserve that heritage: some of the old photographs published here, reproduced from fading prints in the Society's archives, illustrate—perhaps for the last time—the lost furniture of vanished palaces.

I have attempted to check the present locations of all pieces mentioned in the text, but because some of them have passed through many hands, this was not always possible. (Just before the book went on press, for example, I learned that the entire Spanish furniture collection of the Buffalo Historical Society, which is mentioned several times in the text, has been sent on permanent loan to the museum of the St. Augustine Society, in the city of St. Augustine, Florida.) Similarly it was not often possible to obtain the dimensions of the pieces (except for those in the Society's collection), but I have included them when available. I have expanded the list of references to include books published since the first edition. These entries indicate a growing scholarly interest in the furniture of Portugal and Latin America. It is hoped that the second edition will prove useful both to scholars and to the designers, dealers and collectors who are responsible for the current revival of enthusiasm for the furniture of Spain.

I wish to add my gratitude for the aid and council given me by the late Archer Milton Huntington, founder and former President of the Hispanic Society; and to thank Mr. A. Hyatt Mayor and the members of the Society's staff for their interest and assistance.

G. H. B.
March, 1964

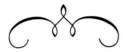

ILLUSTRATIONS

xi

ILLUSTRATIONS

Chests

ILLUSTRATIONS

Vargueños

ILLUSTRATIONS

CONTENTS

SPANISH GOTHIC FURNITURE

SPAIN rose from a group of separate states into a strong, centralized nation during the fifteenth century. Internal warfare ceased after the fall of Granada, and reforms instituted by the Catholic Kings brought order, security, and prosperity to the Spanish people. Crowning the remarkable achievements of this century was the discovery of America with its promise of inestimable wealth and opportunity for the future.

Few examples of domestic furniture built earlier than the fifteenth century, and particularly before the reign of Ferdinand and Isabel, have survived. Not only decay, but also neglect, fire and pillage have taken their toll of pieces which furnished mediæval mansions.

Late Gothic Spanish furniture is similar to that of the rest of Christian Europe. Ornament, largely influenced by Northern ecclesiastical architecture, is French, Flemish, and German in design. Ironwork, especially large-headed nails or bosses, and the combining of Muhammadan with Christian design in a style called *mudéjar* are characteristic of Spanish joinery. The predominant qualities are massiveness, dignity, splendour of material, and honest construction which is stronger but less finished than that of France or Italy.

Abundance, strength, and smooth beauty of warm-coloured walnut wood made it a favourite with Spanish artisans for many centuries. Although it is an ideal material for furniture, its susceptibility to worm and decay has caused the destruction of much Gothic and Renaissance woodwork. Second in importance was the tougher, less plastic oak, the popularity of which waned during the sixteenth century. Chestnut, poplar, and pine were also furniture woods.

Furniture makers in Spain, during the fifteenth century, were members of the carpenters' guild which, despite strict municipal and royal supervision, was a thriving organization. It included turners, sawyers,

FIGURE I

CARPENTER'S
BENCH
AND TOOLS

From the XV century
painting *Casa Santa,* by
Martín Torner in the
Vilallonga Mir Collection,
Palma de Mallorca

and all other artisans who worked with wood, such as makers of decorative Moorish ceilings, of standards and shields for joust and battle, of musical instruments, and of leather-seated chairs (1). Many of these groups, among them turners and chair makers, were to break away during the following century and form guilds of their own (2), but cabinetmakers did not develop an independent organization until the end of the seventeenth century (3).

The carpenters' guild possessed its own charter and statutes, its meeting house, its coat of arms and banner displaying the emblems of the craft, the saw and axe, and its *cofradía* or religious and charitable brotherhood under the protection of Saint Joseph (4). In addition to regulating the production and sale of goods, the association cared for the artisan in sickness and misfortune (5).

In the kingdom of Aragón, during the fifteenth century, furniture makers were named *caixers* as opposed to *bosquers* who constructed ceilings, doors, and other architectural features, or *capsers* who built undecorated boxes (6). Laws controlling the products of these craftsmen were especially severe under the Catholic Kings who tried to unify the guilds by determining design, material, method of work, and price. As a result, tradition was maintained, quality was good, but individual creative ability was stifled.

2

That jealousy and rivalry existed between wood-working organizations of the different Spanish cities is shown by an ordinance issued by Valencian carpenters in 1482 prohibiting carved chests made in Barcelona from entering Valencia, with the boast that Barcelona's chests were no better than Valencia's. Such laws do not seem to have been effective, for in 1497 another attempt was made in Valencia to keep out products of carpentry from Cataluña, Castilla, and other parts of the Peninsula (7).

The artisan who wished to become a master craftsman, with the privilege of opening a shop where furniture could be sold, began his career by serving as an apprentice for four years in the establishment of a master by whom he was fed and clothed and taught the use of saw, axe, hammer, chisel, and plane (8). This apprenticeship was followed by a period of three years as a trained workman or journeyman paid by the day. After 1460 the journeyman was required to pass an examination and construct a test piece which was judged by a committee of officials of the guild (9). It was also necessary to pay a fee to the treasurer, amounting in Valencia, at this time, to fifty *sueldos* for natives and a hundred for foreigners (10). Special privileges and exceptions to the ordinances were granted sons of masters in order that they be encouraged to perpetuate the craftsmanship and guild spirit of their families. The way was also made easier for the journeyman who married the daughter or widow of a master (11).

A fifteenth-century carpenter is shown at work in a primitive painting, *Casa Santa*, by Martín Torner in the Vilallonga Mir Collection, Palma de Mallorca (Fig. 1). The subject of the painting is the home at Nazareth but the interpretation that of Gothic Spain. Saint Joseph stands amid the tools of his craft, holding a plane in his hand. Against the workbench before him leans a bucksaw, which differs little from those in use to-day,

FIGURE 2

CARPENTER'S
BENCH
AND TOOLS
Detail from a XV century
illuminated *Book of Hours*
in the Museo Episcopal,
Vich

3

FIGURE 3

GOTHIC CHEST
XV century. In the Museo
Episcopal, Vich

and an axe with a long, curved handle. Among the scattered tools it is
possible to identify a compass or dividers, an auger, pincers, a mallet,
claw hammer, and an instrument with wooden handle and long blade
which appears to be a kind of chisel. At his left are boxes strewn with
large iron nails. Across the room the Virgin is seated upon a cushioned
stool, busy at a loom decorated with crocketed spires. The Christ Child,
in the foreground of the picture, holds up a wooden bar on a cord.

An illumination from a manuscript of the same period and subject
also pictures carpenters' tools (Fig. 2). Here appear a hatchet instead
of an axe and a smaller kind of saw.

Among the articles produced by fifteenth-century carpenters, that
used more than any other, and by all kinds of people, was the chest.
It could serve not only for the storage of such equipment as clothes,
money, arms, food, books, and other personal property, but also for a
seat, table, sideboard, trunk, and even bed. Sizes and shapes varied,
ranging from small table caskets for jewels and trinkets to massive
wardrobes. The most splendid chests were destined to hold the gala
dress of courtiers and ladies of fashion, or the valuable presents received
by brides. Extravagance to the point of folly was expressed in the
costumes and accessories packed away to be exhibited with pomp and

4

show at banquets, jousts, bullfights, processions, and all ceremonious occasions (12).

Designs on painted and gilded, inlaid, or carved chests were usually either geometric or religious (Figs. 3–5). Battle and hunting scenes and pictures from metrical romances were popular subjects, as were heraldic emblems, Gothic symbols, and inscriptions.

Since chests were the most useful pieces of furniture, they were carefully preserved and now outnumber other existing household goods of the fifteenth century. From this period comes a small Castilian jewel box of walnut (S78, Fig. 118) in the collection of the Hispanic Society. Bird and animal grotesques amid tangled foliage, vine work, human heads, and nude boys are deeply cut in the Flemish-Burgundian tradition. The mouldings are rough and extremely simple. The crosses fleury on the first and fourth quarters of an escutcheon indicate that the box belonged to a member or chapter of the military order of Calatrava or of Alcántara. Lack of any trace of colour makes it impossible to tell whether they are the red of the former or green of the latter. The casket's shape is copied from early Gothic tombs which so often had peaked roofs and rested upon animal supports. Around the truncated top of the

FIGURE 4

LID OF A CHEST
Inlaid lid of a XV century Hispano-Moresque chest in the Victoria and Albert Museum, London

FIGURE 5

MUDÉJAR CHEST

XV-XVI century chest in
the Museo Nacional de
Artes Decorativas, Madrid

lid runs a prayer in Latin to Saint Eustace, patron of hunters.

Another piece of Gothic furniture (S58, Fig. 119) in the Society's collection, which dates from the end of the century, is a rectangular *cofre* with convex lid, covered with crimson velvet and mounted with flamboyant ironwork. Probably a wedding chest which contained the trousseau of a wealthy bride, its principal interest lies in the ironwork with lacelike, double tracery, crocketed pinnacles, and square shell locks. Mountings of this pattern were greatly favoured by ironsmiths during the time of the Catholic Kings. Because a box thus reënforced is practically indestructible, an unusual number of such pieces have been preserved in Spanish museums and private collections. The Royal Ontario Museum of Archaeology, Toronto, and the Buffalo Historical Society possess examples of this type of chest but the decorative shell locks and hasps of the chest at Buffalo are missing.

At The Metropolitan Museum of Art, New York, there are two leather-covered Gothic chests with iron mounts like those on S58. One with a flat lid and central handle was probably used as a strong box for money and papers. Such strong boxes often had several locks with stout hasps and, as a further precaution, were sometimes made entirely of iron.

Two handsome fifteenth-century Gothic chests in American museums are those at The Isabella Stewart Gardner Museum, Boston, and the Rhode Island School of Design, Providence (Figs. 6 and 7). On each, the fenestral ogival tracery is deeply cut and framed in the Spanish fashion by flat stiles and rails instead of by mouldings. The carving which decorates the panels of the Boston chest is varied in pattern and delicate in execution. The elaborate square lock is a notable example of the fifteenth-century ironsmith's art. This chest bears the arms of Rodrigo de Velasco, bishop of Palencia, who died in 1485.

It is possible to learn something about Spanish household goods made by carpenters for fifteenth-century dwellings from such sources as primitive paintings, illustrations in manuscripts and books, carvings, and inventories of possessions, which not only list but in some cases describe the objects. In studying pictorial examples, it is wise to consider types which appear again and again in works by well-known Spanish artists or members of their schools, from different parts of the Peninsula. Otherwise, an individual piece may be the mere whim of an artist's fancy or the memory picture of a foreigner. Fortunately, the Spaniard's desire for realism compelled him to paint what he saw before his eyes.

Among the inventories made for kings, nobles, and clergy, an interesting list dated 1451 contains the equipment of the Castle of Peñíscola, then owned by the military order of Montesa (13). Each section and room of the stronghold has been named and its contents itemized. The main chamber was furnished with a bed having two posts and eight cross boards, straw mattress, and coverings, and another bed, probably used by a servant, which was corded and placed below the larger. This room also contained a joined bench, a painted chest fitted with a lock, and two wooden tables.

Most fifteenth-century beds of state were supported by platforms made of low chests serving as seats or as steps. Such pieces were surmounted by canopies, fastened to the backboards or wall, which overhung the entire bed, and were upheld at the front by cords attached to the ceiling. Footboards and their posts are rarely portrayed during

FIGURE 6

GOTHIC OAK CHEST
XV century. In the
Isabella Stewart Gardner
Museum, Boston

this period. From the canopies were suspended hangings which could be looped up in the daytime.

A detail of a primitive painting by the Vergós family, *The Birth of Saint Stephen*, contains one of the finest examples of the late Gothic bed of state (Fig. 8). The chest fronts forming the dais are crisply moulded and cut with ogival designs, and each compartment has a lock. In front of the bed is a cradle on rockers in which sleeps a small demon who has been substituted for the baby saint. A bed very like this appears in the panel, *The Birth of the Virgin*, painted by the Aragonese Jaime Lana in 1492. Its chest base is also decorated with clearly defined mouldings. In this picture there is an iron brazier, an object used for heating purposes throughout Spain from the most ancient times to the present day. Another kind of canopy for the bed of state was shaped like a tent and was hung from the ceiling over the centre. An example is seen at the upper left of the Castilian *retablo*, *The Annunciation* (A13) at the Hispanic Society. This primitive also depicts a lectern or tall stool elaborately carved with ogives.

A canopied bed showing a sling for holding up the hangings appears in *El libro de proprietatibus rerum*, a Spanish translation by Vicente de Burgos of the Latin by Bartholomaeus Glanville *anglicus*, 1494 (Fig. 9). In this scene a doctor administers medicine to his patient within a bedroom shown next door to an apothecary's shop.

FIGURE 7

GOTHIC WALNUT CHEST

XV century. At the Rhode Island School of Design, Providence

FIGURE 8

BED AND CRADLE
XV century. A panel from
the *Retablo of Saint Stephen
of Granollers* by the Vergós
family in the Museo de
Arte de Cataluña,
Barcelona

9

FIGURE 9

CANOPIED BED
XV century. From a
woodcut in *El libro de
proprietatibus rerum* by
Bartholomaeus Glanville,
anglicus, printed in
Tholosa in 1494

The great kitchen in the Castle of Peñíscola contained a wooden cabinet or *armario* which was fastened to the wall, a throne chair, a bench, and a table. The remaining rooms of the building were sparsely furnished with joined beds, various kinds of chests, tables and benches. The only chairs mentioned were one in the kitchen and four in the church, chests, stools, benches, and cushions evidently being used in place of them for seats.

In Spain, and indeed in other European countries at this time, it was customary for the head of a wealthy household to possess the only armchair, with possibly a few smaller chairs to be offered to the most distinguished guests, a gesture conveying great honour. The master's chair was often similar to the elaborately carved bishops' thrones of churches. An example of this type of chair is to be seen in the background of an Hispano-Flemish panel in the Prado, showing the beheading of Saint John the Baptist (Fig. 10). The canopy and the back of the seat are hung with a large-patterned cloth of honour, the sides are carved in the Gothic style with ogives, and the heavy base was probably fitted with a chest, as was customary for such pieces.

An upholstered chair of state is mentioned in the incomplete inventory

10

of goods (1412–1424) of Alfonso the Fifth of Aragón, as prince and king, the term "upholstered" being used here merely to indicate cloth coverings over the wood or hung from the supports. The chair is described as fitted with green velvet, trimmed with green fringe, and decorated with the royal arms and those of Sicily. Among the Monarch's possessions are also listed a variety of chests and boxes as well as four secretaries or cabinets which were even more rare in Spain than fine chairs during the Gothic period (14). The name of the King's carpenter, Pascual Esteve, has been preserved. In 1440 Esteve was charged with the construction of a number of works of wood including a paneled chamber, a table, benches, a lectern, and a bed with a large red canopy topped by a gilded copper ball (15).

Apart from throne chairs, two other important seats were the new hip-joint chair or *sillón de cadera* and the old form of scissors chair. Prototypes of these pieces were popular in Italy, where they have been named for Dante and Savonarola respectively. The frames of the hip-joint chairs were of tangent, pivoted semi-circles, one set forming the

FIGURE 10

THRONE CHAIR
XV century. Detail from an Hispano-Flemish panel showing the beheading of Saint John the Baptist. In the Museo Nacional del Prado, Madrid

legs and the other the framework of the seat. An example with seat and back hung with cloth or leather attached by nails is carved on the pulpit of the Palencia Cathedral (Fig. 13). Although the panel was made during the sixteenth century, the chair is of the previous century in style. A bishop seated in the chair is writing at a lectern or desk decorated with Renaissance motives but shaped at the front with Gothic linen fold, a design rarely seen in Spanish woodwork except on pieces showing Flemish characteristics. In localities where Moorish designs persisted, the frames of hip-joint chairs were often covered with geometric ivory inlay. Two armchairs illustrating such work are at the Victoria and Albert Museum, London, and the *Kunstgewerbemuseum*, Cologne.

Hip-joint, scissors, and X-shaped stools were made so that they could be folded and carried on mule back from place to place, a measure which the scarcity of decorative furniture demanded (Figs. 11, 12).

Large benches, sometimes built into the paneling of the wall, were also considered seats of honour during this century. Their decoration was

FIGURE 11

HIP-JOINT CHAIR
XV century inlaid chair in the collection of the Städtisches Kunstgewerbe Museum, Cologne

FIGURE 12

HIP-JOINT CHAIR
XV century. In the
Plandiura Collection,
Barcelona

copied from that of ecclesiastical stalls, and their bases usually enclosed chests.

Desks were of two kinds: one a low, detached piece of furniture with shelf below, and the other a heavier piece often built into the wall with manuscript shelves above. A representation of the built-in type of desk is engraved on the arm of a rare and handsome crucifix, called that of Santa Eulalia, made by Francisco Vilardell, and now in the Cathedral at Barcelona (Fig. 14). The crucifix is dated 1383, but this type of desk continued to be made throughout the fifteenth century.

A panel from the *retablo* of *Saint John the Baptist*, Catalan School,

13

fifteenth century, shows Zacharias seated upon a chest-bench before a desk on which he is writing the name of John (Fig. 15). Back and canopy of the bench are carved with foliations and the top crested with *fleurons*. The desk is made of plain boards, the ends cut with pointed openings, and the dovetailing of the sides left visible. A raised edge at the front braces the inclined writing board. In this provincial picture are depicted the two main characteristics of Spanish woodwork, strength and magnificence.

Undecorated low benches, long boards on trestle or peg legs, were commonly used, especially at table, along with stools of the same type. Gothic tables consisted of removable planks set upon trestles. A table of this kind with trestles cusped in trefoil designs appears in an early fifteenth-century panel of the Catalan School entitled *The Last Supper* (Fig. 16). The diners are placed at one side of the table with Christ at the centre seated upon a large throne. A later portrayal of *The Last Supper* in *Thesoro de la pasion sacratissimo* by Andres de Li, printed at Burgos in 1493, pictures boxlike stools with cusped ends.

Another piece of furniture used in connection with dining was the sideboard for serving food or displaying prized possessions, such as plate

FIGURE 13

DESK AND CHAIR
XV century in style.
Carved on the pulpit of
the Cathedral at Palencia

FIGURE 14

DESK AND CHAIR
XIV-XV century. Detail
of a silver crucifix made
by Francisco Vilardell, in
the Cathedral at Barcelona

or pottery. An unusually elaborate, canopied example is shown in a painting of *The Annunciation* finished in 1475 by Pedro de Córdoba, in which there is also a prayer desk with a cabinet base (Fig. 17).

Among the inventories of household goods belonging to commoners, those drawn up at Barcelona by the notaries Bartomeu Costa, 1455–1467, and Galcerán Balaguer, late fifteenth century, have been preserved to the present day (16). The belongings of such men as merchants, money brokers, apothecaries, and surgeons are represented in these documents. Their goods were few, but the ownership of even a small number of decorative pieces shows the increased prosperity of men of

15

FIGURE 15

DESK AND BENCH

XV century. Panel from
the *Retablo of Saint John
the Baptist* by Pedro
García de Benabarre in the
Museo de Arte de
Cataluña, Barcelona

16

middle rank who rivaled the upper classes politically and strove to outdo them in power. The objects most frequently mentioned are chests, usually painted and fitted with a lock, a number of which are described as being Valencian. Tables are listed, one made to be used for playing chess, and also benches, either small for seats at table or larger with chests or drawers inside. The widow of Bartomeu Gualbes owned four folding chairs, the only chairs mentioned, a black and yellow bench with drawers, and two coffers of Valencian work. One bed appears, that of Joan Berenguer de Junyent, which was a wooden joined bed with two chests having locks built into it. This man also owned the only cabinet spoken of, made of poplar, as well as two coffers and a pine chest.

An inventory of late Gothic furniture which has come to light, unusual in the amount of goods possessed by a person without rank, is that of Doctor Jaime Torres, including household equipment to the value of fourteen thousand Valencian *sueldos*, which he gave to his wife, Esperanza Salvador, according to their marriage contract on June 14th, 1504 (17). An indication of his wealth is his library of seventy-five manuscripts and books on medicine and art, a most imposing amount of literature to be held by a private individual during the fifteenth century. Seats listed in the inventory consist of six benches, two being fitted with drawers, and a half dozen stools. Of beds there are four with their mattresses and accessories. Other objects are a table, four coffers painted red and gold, three very small coffers, and six chests, one from Barcelona, one described as being oak, three as very small, and one to be used for

FIGURE 16

TRESTLE TABLE

XV century. Detail of a panel of the Catalan School entitled *The Last Supper*, by Jaime Ferrer I, in the Museo Diocesano, Solsona. (Large dark rectangle in foreground is the back of a chair that was clumsily retouched out of the negative.)

FIGURE 17

SIDEBOARD
AND
DESK

XV century. In a painting
entitled *The Annunciation
with Saints and Donors,* by
Pedro de Córdoba, in the
Cathedral at Córdoba

writing. Chairs and cabinets are not mentioned.

From the sources presented it has been possible to list the kinds of
furniture in use at the beginning of the Renaissance as beds, tables,
chairs, benches, stools, chests of every description, desks or lecterns,
cabinets, and sideboards. These items continued to be made throughout
the sixteenth century, their number and sumptuousness growing along
with the increased security and wealth of the country.

18

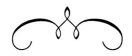

THE RENAISSANCE

UNDER the Catholic Kings, Spain had become a first-class power, although the final barriers of mediæval seclusion were not broken down until the reign of their grandson Charles the Fifth. Heritage and conquest provided this monarch not only with Spain but also with the Netherlands, most of the Italian peninsula, lands on the Danube, and vast territories in the New World. A Burgundian who became more sympathetic with the Spanish point of view as time went on, Charles advanced Spain's prestige farther into western Europe than ever before and, in England, placed his son on the throne as King Consort from 1553 to 1558. Revenues of gold and silver from the Indies, which poured in during the late forties and fifties, made Spain the spearhead of Hapsburg imperialism, supporting wars against Protestants and Muhammadans. About the middle of the century, Spain reached the height of her power as the greatest state in Europe. After the abdication of Charles in 1558, Philip the Second, who was Spanish by birth and inclination, received all of his father's acquisitions except the Hapsburg territory on the Rhine and Danube. He spent his own reign, which lasted until 1598, striving to maintain the possessions and religion of his Catholic country.

II

During this most glorious century in Spain's history, a period of political consolidation at home and conquest abroad, all the arts flourished under the guardianship of both Charles and Philip and of their courts which fostered artistic endeavour. The Burgundian form of court had been introduced into Spain by Charles the Fifth and adapted by Philip as prince and king. It was more ceremonious, ostentatious, and costly than the simple but well-liked Castilian model.

Growth of prosperity during this century became apparent in the erection of public buildings, palaces, and monuments and also in the finer town dwellings of the middle class. Furniture design, as in the past, followed the lead of architecture, becoming Renaissance in accordance with the new style which arrived from Italy.

19

After a transitional period of mingling with the Gothic, chaste plant forms, ogives, and foils gave way entirely to intricate and minute ornament which has been named plateresque from its resemblance to the delicate work of the silversmith. Such ornament was made of classical heads in wreaths, cherubs, urns, trophies, masks, birds, grotesque half figures, or animal forms in lively action. Its adaptation to furniture is shown on the doors of a sacristy wardrobe in the anteroom of the chapter house at Toledo Cathedral, carved in 1549 by Gregorio Pardo (Fig. 18). Another example of Renaissance carving on furniture is that decorating a cabinet for vestments in the sacristy of the Church of *San Pedro*, Ubeda, Jaén. Plateresque ornament increased in elaboration and exuberance until the latter part of the century when Philip the Second banished it in favour of the severe classic style more in accord

FIGURE 18

RENAISSANCE
CARVING

Door of a XVI century
wardrobe in the Cathedral
at Toledo

with his temperament, known as Herreran from its exponent, Juan de Herrera, state architect.

After the end of racial wars in Spain and of struggles between great feudal lords whose power was finally subordinated to that of the king, many nobles left their mediæval fortresses and moved into towns. Here they built palaces, usually of two stories, with bleak stone facades spotted with rich ornament, around intricately carved open *patios*, which had two orders of covered galleries joined by a broad stair. The plan of the Spanish town mansion seldom varied after this century and has been used in much the same way up to the present time. On the ground floor was the *recibidor*, the only master's room, the rest being given over to servants and animals. The main floor had boxlike apartments customarily beautified by carved wooden doors and ceilings,

FIGURE 19

CANOPIED BED
A XVI century bed depicted on a carved poplar panel entitled *The Birth of the Virgin;* in the collection of the Hispanic Society of America, New York

FIGURE 20

FOLDING BENCH
Late XVI or early XVII
century leather-covered
bench at the Museo
Arqueológico Nacional,
Madrid

dados of polychrome tiles, carved plaster frames around windows and doorways, and tapestries or gilded leather hangings. The *salon*, the largest room, possibly contained a dais, but one room was very like another, since built-in furnishings were seldom used after Gothic days.

The kind of household equipment owned by the great lords may be determined from such an inventory as that of the third Duke of Alburquerque, dated 1560, enumerating the most interesting and valuable articles in the historic castle at Cuéllar (18). This wealthy and powerful duke, who served so valorously under Charles the Fifth, owned several very splendid beds. They are described as having canopies, hangings, valances, spreads, and other accessories of velvet, scarlet cloth of Toledo and Sevilla, silk, damask, Turkish cloth, serge, painted and worked linen, or network from Rouen. When not red, the colours of the hangings were black, yellow, or green. Trimmings consisted of twisted silk or wool fringe, braid, and silver embroidery. In value these magnificent beds were estimated to run as high as one hundred and ten ducats. The inventory gives very little information about their frames, merely listing some as made of poplar, walnut, oak, or pine. Trunks were provided to hold the draperies of a few of these pieces. A pine trundle-bed on castors, four plain, corded beds on which the pages slept, and six pine benches used as beds by servants are also listed.

During the Renaissance, bed canopies were no longer hung from the ceiling at one end but were supported by posts at the four corners. These posts were fluted and carved, or turned in columnar form, topped by more or less elaborate finials. Carved Renaissance motives replaced Gothic paneling on the headboards. A bed with its draperies looped up exposing the posts is carved in high relief on a sixteenth-century poplar panel, *The Birth of the Virgin* (D47), in the collection of The Hispanic Society of America (Fig. 19). The relief also shows a little stand with trestle supports and an old-fashioned Gothic-type stool. Another example of the poster bed, with undecorated frame, is that of Philip the Second at the Escorial. It stands upon a low dais covered with Cordovan leather. This bed, very plain in comparison with many owned by the King's subjects, is hung with red silk, banded with yellow brocade and lined with yellow silk. Severe and dignified furniture of this kind was very pleasing to Philip during the latter part of his life. Among the beds which he is known to have occupied was one at the house of the Licenciate Lugo at Salamanca where, as a prince, he awaited his Portuguese bride (19). It was upheld by a dais covered and hung with cloth of gold, spread with a silver coverlet embroidered with gold, and surrounded by a silver railing. Near at hand stood a silver table and brazier, suitable furniture for the future monarch. Tables and table covers are listed among the

FIGURE 21

SACRISTY BENCH
Velvet-covered XVI century bench from Palencia Cathedral, at the Montreal Museum of Fine Arts

23

Duke of Alburquerque's possessions, the latter made of velvet, taffeta, fine scarlet cloth of Valencia, or green woolen of Cuenca. A painting of Saint Ildefonso by El Greco shows the beauty of such covers. Embroidered, fringed, and fastened with gold frogs, they hid the woodwork completely.

An example of the silver furniture which was so popular during this century is a small table bordered and ornamented with silver, bearing the arms of the Duke and Duchess (20). The application of silver to furniture grew so prevalent that later both Philip the Second and his successor, in order to overcome frauds and to avoid waste, had to promulgate sumptuary laws in 1593 and 1600 prohibiting or limiting its use in connection with furniture. These laws were not entirely effective (21). The silver furniture of Antonio Pérez, unfortunate secretary to Philip the Second, is well known. It consisted of beds, chairs, braziers, coffers, and tables. One brazier was estimated to be worth sixty thousand ducats, and a carved silver mirror set with pearls and gems was considered unique. The master's bed had silver angels on top of its posts as finials and bore an inscription which read, "Antonio Pérez sleeps, tread softly." The contents of this house at Madrid became so luxurious that guests were asked to remove their shoes upon entering, as did Moors before going into a holy place. After the overthrow of the Secretary of State the furnishings were destined to fall under the auctioneer's hammer

FIGURE 22

FOLDING CHAIR (*left*)
XVI century armchair in the Museo Episcopal, Vich

FIGURE 23

ARMCHAIR (*right*)
XVI-XVII century walnut chair with velvet upholstery in the Victoria and Albert Museum, London

for a fraction of their worth (22).

The number of chairs used in the castle at Cuéllar shows that seating furniture was no longer so scarce as it had been during the previous century. More than ten hip-joint chairs, four chairs with baluster backs, four chairs called Flemish with black leather seats and backs, hinged for folding, as well as a sedan of yew in which the Duke was accustomed to ride, are listed. Among the hip-joint chairs, the majority of which were inlaid with ivory, one, described as upholstered in green velvet trimmed with twisted silk fringe, fastened by gilded nails, and another similar low chair were designated for ladies. Gentlewomen, however, still used cushions in the Moorish fashion rather than chairs to a great extent. The frames of these chairs were walnut, beech, or orange wood. Among the benches were three with ironwork, which could be folded up and taken on journeys, and a number of table benches, sometimes fastened to the table by a chain, and often containing a chest for clothing or hangings (23). A bench illustrating the leather-covered folding type is in the *Museo Arqueológico Nacional*, Madrid. The shaping of its removable legs and iron braces places it as a late example, perhaps made in the seventeenth century (Fig. 20). Velvet was a popular upholstery for benches during the Renaissance. At the Art Association of Montreal

FIGURE 26

ARMCHAIR (*left*)
XVI century walnut chair
with embossed leather
upholstery; in The
Metropolitan Museum of
Art, New York

FIGURE 27

ARMCHAIR (*right*)
XVI-XVII walnut chair
with leather back and seat.
In the collection of E. T.
Guymon, Jr., San Diego

there is a sixteenth-century church bench from the Cathedral of Palencia
with the original fringed and nail-studded velvet (Fig. 21).

As shown by the inventory, the hip-joint was the most popular chair
during the first half of the sixteenth century. Large seats of state similar
to Gothic examples but carved with Renaissance designs in the tradition
of Siloe and Berruguete also appeared. An X-stool, said to have been
used by Charles the Fifth and still preserved in the apartments of

FIGURE 28

CHINESE CHAIRS
XVI century monk's chair
and two antique Chinese
yoke-backed chairs in
Philip II's room in the
Escorial

Philip the Second at the Escorial, is a sixteenth-century type of seat which recalls the furniture of ancient Rome. It rests upon cloven hoofs, but the seat-supports are finished with carved leafage instead of animal heads. The joints between seat and legs are faced with lion masks, and the seat is fitted with a tasseled velvet cushion.

Characteristic of the Renaissance was the rectangular chair hung with leather attached by large nail heads, which came in about the middle of the century. This seat, peculiarly Spanish in upholstery and metal work, had a medium high back, slightly raked back posts topped with bracket-shaped, scrolled-leaf, or metal ball finials, and rather narrow, sloping or straight arms with scrolled over ends. The legs, continuing at the front to form arm supports, were usually connected with plain, low side and back stretchers, and at the front with a high, wide stretcher either fretted or carved with Renaissance motives or ornamental coats of arms. Armorial bearings usually appeared on the upholstery as well as on the front stretcher.

Rectangular armchairs are now called *sillones fraileros* or monks' chairs from their general use in monasteries. Matching side chairs were also built. Many armchairs were constructed in such a way that they could be folded for traveling, but later, when their upholstery was no longer hung but firmly attached to the four seat rails, this construction was not possible. An early example of the folding chair at the Vich

FIGURE 29

SEDAN CHAIR
XVI century leather-
covered sedan chair in
the Escorial

FIGURE 30

CATALAN CHEST

XVI century painted and gilded bride's chest in The Cleveland Museum of Art

Museum has runner feet, a feature more often seen on Italian than Spanish chairs (Fig. 22). It is upholstered with modern velvet and both stretchers and legs are hinged. The early date of this chair is indicated by the fretting of the stretchers, on which the Gothic foil is suggested.

Leather upholstery for monks' chairs, usually of calf which became especially tough after tanning, was sometimes plain or sometimes stitched in geometric patterns. The favourite upholstery was the intricately designed *guadamecil*, a kind of worked leather originally made by the Moors, with patterns in relief raised by pressure and often brilliantly coloured or embossed with gold or silver (24). Centres for building chairs with *guadameciles* were, with Córdoba leading, Barcelona, Sevilla, and other leather-manufacturing cities of the Peninsula. Doménech and Pérez Bueno state that similar chairs in Italy, France, England, Germany, and the Low Countries were due to Spanish influence, there being a great exportation of leather-seated chairs from Spanish workshops to these countries (25). Chairs of rectangular form usually upholstered with fringed velvet or brocade appear in portraits painted by such artists as El Greco, Antonio Moro, and González. In a portrait of Philip's daughter, Isabella Clara Eugenia, by Sánchez Coello, the entire frame is ornamented by bandings or fillets. The back posts are finished with metal ball finials, and the velvet upholstery, bordered with braid and heavy fringe, is attached to the frame by gilded nails. The velvet is fastened to

FIGURE 31

CATALAN CHEST
XVI century painted and gilded groom's chest in the Museo Episcopal, Vich

FIGURE 32

MUDÉJAR CHEST
Miniature XVI century inlaid chest 13 cm. high by 29 cm. wide (approximately 5 by 11½ inches); in the Museo Episcopal, Vich

FIGURE 33

CATALAN CHEST

XVI century inlaid nuptial chest in the Museo Balaguer, Villanueva y Geltrú

the rear of the back posts instead of the front, a style called *a maderas vistas* or "with the wood exposed" (26).

An armchair at the Victoria and Albert Museum, (Fig. 23), said to have come from the Palace of the Archbishop of Toledo, differs from the usual form in having caryatids for arm supports. The chair's velvet upholstery is quilted, embroidered, and fringed, and is attached by ornate bosses. Other fine chairs of the period appear in Figs. 24–27.

At the Escorial there are a number of monks' chairs. Those in the apartments of Philip the Second are plain with leather upholstery, and those in the rooms of the Infanta Isabella Clara Eugenia are also plain but richer in appearance with their fringed and embroidered velvet coverings and elaborate pillows. In Philip's room stand two folding Chinese chairs which were used by the King as leg rests (Fig. 28). These yoke-backed chairs were great curiosities during the sixteenth century.

Another interesting piece of furniture in this room is a sedan made of a leather-seated armchair with a high frame to uphold a canopy and curtains, a foot rest, and metal grips on the leg posts through which staves for carrying could be slid (Fig. 29). A chair of this kind is listed in an inventory of the goods of Charles the Fifth in his retreat at Yuste

30

(27). In such a sedan, Philip the Second, who superintended as much as possible of the building of the Escorial, his grim monastery and palace, was carried up into the mountains to a stone seat which overlooked the vast project (28). Three late-sixteenth or early-seventeenth century chairs (S15, Fig. 120) at the Hispanic Society are similar in framework to the *sillones fraileros* at the Escorial. These have high, wide back and front stretchers, bracket-shaped at the lower corners, like the stretchers on a number of chairs in the apartments of Philip the Second. Plainer, sturdier frames can hardly be imagined, the chairs depending entirely upon their upholstery for decoration.

The only chests appearing in the Duke of Alburquerque's inventory are ten simple pine boxes, with locks, to hold ten tapestry panels depicting the history of Abraham (29). But the Duke must have owned a great number of chests to safeguard his gold and silver plate, jewelry, chapel treasures, clothing, hangings, and other valuable possessions. Such chests would have been similar to those built at the close of the fifteenth century, but with Renaissance designs for carving, painting, inlay, metal work, cloth, or embossed leather. The great, carved walnut examples with portrait medallions, trophies, and other classical motives

FIGURE 34

CATALAN CHEST
XVI century bride's chest painted, and carved with plateresque designs in a private collection at Barcelona

31

were apt to have more elaborate mouldings than Gothic pieces, the egg and dart, acanthus, and dentil being especially popular. Decorative single-hasped locks remained in style, but heavy iron strappings and bandings went out. Miniature models of large chests were used as jewel caskets or table boxes. A type of chest differing from all others and constructed in Spain only in the region of Cataluña appeared at the turn of the fifteenth to the sixteenth century. At one side of its face was a door which concealed a set of drawers to hold small articles. Both inner and outer sides of the lid were decorated, the inner usually painted with religious scenes. Sometimes an extra lid was provided to protect the contents when the top was lifted back against the wall. These boxes with drawers are called brides' chests or *hembras*, while their companion pieces, which differ only in their lack of door and drawers, are grooms' chests or *machos* (30). An early, painted and gilded nuptial chest carved with Gothic tracery at The Cleveland Museum of Art is an excellent example of the Catalan form (Fig. 30). A similarly decorated *macho* is in the Vich Museum (Fig. 31).

Despite the fall of the Moorish kingdom in 1492, Muhammadan design continued to have great influence over Spanish art and decoration. The conquered Moorish artisans, working for Christians until their final expulsion in 1609, produced that mingling of Asiatic and European

FIGURE 35

PLATERESQUE
VARGUEÑO

XVI century. In the
Segraneda Collection,
Palma de Mallorca

FIGURE 36

INLAID VARGUEÑO
XVI century. In the
Österreichisches Museum
für Angewandte Kunst,
Vienna

construction and ornamentation which made up the previously mentioned *mudéjar* style. Lack of trees in the arid countries formerly occupied by this race and the hot climate of southern Spain, which caused large areas of solid wood to split and warp, are reasons why Moorish craftsmen were inclined to use many small bits of wood to make up their doors, ceilings, decorative furniture, and other woodwork. As masters of delicate and complicated joinery these carpenters have never been surpassed. Moorish household goods were more limited in variety and number than those owned by Christians. Representative examples appear to have been inlaid boxlike chests without architectural influence. Fulfilling the Oriental desire for complex and repetitive design leaving no surface unbroken, the decoration of these pieces took the form of small-scale, geometric, ivory, star and flower patterns combined with budded scrolls and *lacería* traced in fine lines of wood. A sixteenth-century *mudéjar* chest at the Vich Museum, although in poor condition, is an illustration of the sturdy construction and elaborate design of such pieces made during the fifteenth, and throughout the sixteenth century (Fig. 32). There is a handsome *mudéjar* inlaid chest at the Hispanic Society (S55, Fig. 121). Around three sides of the interior runs

33

a tier of drawers and lidded boxes. Perhaps this piece served as a trunk for a lady's shawls and mantillas, the drawers holding jewels and trinkets, and the bins, gloves, fans, and ribbons (31). Inlaid furniture was manufactured principally at Granada, Toledo, Zaragoza, Córdoba, Sevilla, Barcelona, and the Balearic Islands, places where members of the conquered race were allowed to live in great numbers. Curiously similar is the inlay of sixteenth-century Italy attributed to Lombardy or to Venice where it was made by the family of Embracchi. Because much of it came from the neighbourhood of Certosa di Pavia it is now called certosina work, but its strong Eastern flavour causes Odom to incline toward a Venetian origin where the influence of Islamic art was great at this time (32).

A piece of furniture which displays the finest type of *mudéjar* inlay is a cabinet at the Hispanic Society (S51, Figs. 123, 124). During the Gothic period, cabinets were extremely rare. They were customarily built into the wall of the castle in the form of arms or food cupboards. Great chests fulfilled practically every storage need until the Renaissance, when portability was no longer so necessary and the convenience of the chest on chest was recognized. The first use of cabinets was in the sacristies of churches where fine examples were placed to hold vestments, sacred vessels, and other objects used during the service. The monogram of Christ traced on the inner side of the top lid of the Society's cabinet indicates that this piece was made for ecclesiastical purposes. The very definite Christian features, leaf moulding, knulling, classical columns, birds, and cherubs' heads on the architectural interior, combined with the Moorish decoration and workmanship, make this cabinet a distinct example of the *mudéjar* style. It is interesting to compare S51 with Fig. 33, one of a pair of Catalan or Mallorcan bridal chests in the collection of the *Museo Balaguer* at Villanueva y Geltrú. These are so similar in construction and decoration as to have been, perhaps, made in the same workshop. The chest illustrated is a groom's chest; its companion piece, not shown, contains a tier of drawers. In simplicity of construction cabinet and chests are alike, with mouldings cut back to frame panels completely filled with myriad bits of ivory or bone. Both have geometric and scrolled *lacería* in fine lines of light wood, although this *lacería* plays a more important part in the design of the cabinet than of the chests. Several of the bone or ivory patterns are identical, and all are similar. Probably the Society's cabinet was originally raised upon feet or a stand as are other pieces of this kind, an example being a

34

FIGURE 37

VARGUEÑO

XVI century cabinet (drop-front missing) with Gothic tracery; in the Städtisches Kunstgewerbe Museum, Cologne

footed *armario* without doors but of nearly the same interior arrangement and inlay in the Lázaro Collection, Madrid. The Lázaro Collection contains also a large sixteenth-century bride's chest with many like features in construction and inlay. Comparison of these chests and cabinets leads one to believe that they came from Cataluña.

The Spanish cabinet writing desk of the Renaissance was the *escritorio*, now called *vargueño*. This modern term has been for some time, and perhaps always will be, an etymological puzzle. The first person to use the word in printed form and to attribute its origin to Vargas, a small town near Toledo, seems to have been Juan Facundo Riaño in 1872. His catalogue of Spanish art objects in the collection of the Victoria and Albert Museum, of this date, contains the following note:

"This is an upper part of a cabinet called in Spain 'Vargueño' from having been generally made at a town called Vargas in the province of Toledo" (33).

The note indicates that the term came to Riaño by word of mouth, which is probably true, for he did not support his statement by documentary proof. So tempting was the Vargas theory that in 1897 it was copied by Davillier (34) and by Miquel y Badía (35), and from then on has been quoted frequently with, apparently, no additional foundation in fact. In 1914 the word *bargueño* with its Vargas derivation was accepted by the Academy dictionary, supported only by traditional use (36). Doménech and Pérez Bueno later denounced the theory and

FIGURE 38

INLAID VARGUEÑO
Second half of XVI century.
In the Victoria and Albert
Museum, London

suggested that the word first came from a sixteenth-century workshop at Toledo, having as its head a master carver and cabinetmaker called Vargas. This opinion, of which no published evidence exists, they state was also held by the late ceramist, Sebastián Aguado (37). Madoz makes no mention of Bargas or Vargas as having been a woodworking centre, an industry he could hardly have overlooked. The products of this little town have long been cereals and oil and the industries, bakeries and oil mills (38).

There seems to be no definite reason to attribute the origin of the *vargueño* cabinet to the vicinity of Toledo rather than to any other centre where the *mudéjar* element, which always influenced its decoration, was strong. The cabinet, an outgrowth of the hutch or treasure chest with drawers, with falling front instead of doors, was set upon either a paneled *armario* stand, called a *taquillón*, or a trestle stand called a *pie de puente*. Both stands were equipped with pulls, usually headed with carved shells, which could be drawn out to support the drop lid of the chest. The *taquillón* may be seen in Fig. 42, and the *pie de puente* in Fig. 41. The *vargueños* in Figs. 142 and 132 show the ultimate or classical form which cabinets took, with their elaborate velvet-backed iron mountings, architecturalized gilded interiors with inlaid lozenges of etched bone, and twisted bone or ivory columns. Such cabinets are more typical of the seventeenth than the sixteenth century, for early chests were plainer and less architectural in design.

A rare and distinctive example of the *vargueño*, puzzling in the problem of its attribution is shown in Fig. 125 (S47). This *vargueño* belongs to a group of pieces decorated with plateresque carvings of close-grained box or fruit wood, backed by cloth. All are so nearly alike that they may have been made at the same place. The existence of an early bridal chest (Fig. 34) in a private collection at Barcelona, which is definitely Catalan in construction and painted decoration, is so similar in carving and metal work as to make it possible to assign this group of cabinets to Cataluña (39). The likeness between the early plateresque *vargueños* and Catalan marriage chests in general and of Fig. 34 in particular, suggests the possibility that *vargueños* originated in the province of Cataluña. One of the finest of the plateresque *vargueños* is the well-known early sixteenth-century example at the Victoria and Albert Museum, London. It has the Moorish-type, inlaid boxwood stringing; openwork of boxwood over red velvet; and inner and outer borders of walnut and pear wood. Another of the group to which S47 belongs is a walnut *vargueño* dated 1530 to 1540 at the *Schlossmuseum*, Berlin, with plateresque boxwood carving over modern salmon-pink rep, and third, a nearly identical piece in the Segraneda Collection, Palma de Mallorca (Fig. 35). There are other such *vargueños* in private collections in Spain. Among the features common to these cabinets are busts of helmeted warriors in silhouette, bead and reel acanthus mouldings, scrolled, foliated and chipped strapwork, confronted chimeric birds, interlaced inlaid stringing, and vase-shaped metal pulls. The early date of these cabinets is shown by the comparatively plain exteriors, lacking, as yet, large pierced iron mountings and the flatness and delicacy of their elaborately carved interiors. A lady's small trinket box with doors opening on a restored interior with drawers, also has boxwood carvings over red silk. This box, formerly in the Almenas Collection, displays many features similar to those of the plateresque *vargueño* cabinets. It is called Aragonese by Byne who compared the warrior-head silhouettes with those on the *patios* of old Zaragozan palaces. While they are somewhat alike, the portrait silhouette was a favourite Renaissance motive and occurs in many other sections of the country (40). The trestle stand of *vargueño* S47 is unusual in that it has lion-head fixed supports instead of pulls, and leonine toes carved at the front of its runners. Legs of *vargueño* stands were copied from the columns of buildings or from spindles of the giant *rejas* in the churches. Turnings of nearly every variety were developed for stands, tables, beds, and chairs during the Renaissance. Stop fluting and spiral reeding were popular treatments for the legs of *vargueño* stands.

Many early *vargueño* cabinets were decorated with inlaid patterns of ivory and light woods. *Vargueño* S42 (Fig. 127) in the Society's collection is an example of this type, but the over-elaboration of its design dates it as near the end of the sixteenth century. Round-arched doors with classic pediments, shell-hooded windows, and the arcaded gallery of the inlaid brick facade on the face of the cabinet point to an Aragonese origin. The knotted rope of Saint Francis forming a border around the lid and the slim crosses between the battlements call attention to the possibility that the cabinet was built for someone connected with the church. Unfortunately the coat of arms at the centre is badly damaged. A comparative piece with urns, scrolled flowers, and classic medallions is at the *Österreichisches Museum für Angewandte Kunst*, in Vienna (Fig. 36). Many other similar *vargueños* are exhibited in Spanish museums and private collections.

38

FIGURE 39

CABINET
XVI century 'Charles the Fifth' cabinet formerly in the Almenas collection

Vargueños of this century were decorated in many different styles. The delicate tracery of Fig. 37 illustrates the lingering influence of the Gothic period, while the inlaid design of Fig. 38 is purely Renaissance.

Another type of cabinet made during the second half of the century was that based on Tuscan models and now called a 'Charles the Fifth'

39

cabinet (41). It consisted of a chest of drawers on a cupboard base, the upper body sometimes having a lid for writing. Distinctive features were pedimented drawers, arcaded panels, tiers of figures, carved nearly in the round arranged as pilasters at the corners, and elaborate friezes and cornices. When built by Spaniards, such cabinets were usually less architectural than foreign examples that closely followed the design of Italian Renaissance buildings (Fig. 39).

Although cabinets are not mentioned in the Duke of Alburquerque's inventory, a later inventory of the goods of Juan de Herrera, architect to Philip the Second, dated March 10th, 1595, lists several including some from Germany (42). Cabinets are also listed in a document of the Royal Procurator at Mallorca, dated 1594 (43). This interesting inventory, by giving the name of each room along with its entire equipment, provides an excellent picture of the sixteenth-century Spanish interior. An example is the chamber of the mistress of the house, having a walnut *bufete* or small table, two beds, one a field bed with posts, made of wood from India, a fine old walnut chest containing textiles, and a large box holding two or three glass figures of Christ, flagons of scent, and some ornaments. Here also was a cabinet on a scissors stand, probably in the form of a *vargueño* without the drop lid, a type now called a *papelera*. Also in the chamber was a dressing case with four drawers holding such things as lace edgings, caps, and collars and a cupboard with many kinds of glassware, pottery, and clothing. A study facing the street contained a walnut chest on a stand, no doubt a *vargueño*, a walnut poster bed, two walnut *bufetes*, and five chairs. Another study looking out on the garden was equipped with a large bookcase and a chest on a stand. The great number of chests, leather-seated chairs, tables, benches, and poster beds in this typical house of an important personage shows the new interest in domestic comfort and reflects the increase of wealth and refinement which had taken place during the Renaissance.

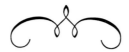

THE SEVENTEENTH CENTURY

AFTER the death of Philip the Second, Spain declined under a succession of weak kings ruled by favourites and was no longer able to hold the leadership of Europe. Continuance of the disastrous foreign policy of war to sustain imperialism exhausted the land to such an extent that it was not able to recover. The seventeenth century was, however, a productive era in æsthetic expression. The decorative as well as the fine arts flourished about the courts of spendthrift monarchs. During the reign of Philip the Fourth, an ardent patron of drama, literature, and art, a reaction set in against the sober Herreran style with its straight lines, plain surfaces, sparse decoration, and massive structure. Baroque design, with movement of line and with ornament which was varied and sometimes excessive, gradually made itself felt, showing increasing extravagance as if in imitation of the court. Unsuccessful attempts, such as the sumptuary law of 1600 (44), were made now and then to control the luxury of furniture and dress, but as long as means or credit could be procured Spaniards made a brilliant outward show to the world.

From this century on, there are other sources of information than inventories and pictorial examples helping to reconstruct the domestic life of Spain (45). Not only do there exist a great many pieces of furniture, but also books of fiction, drama, and even an occasional political treatise describe the goods and customs of the Spanish people. Seventeenth-century authors agree so closely regarding the environment in which their characters moved that their descriptions must be remarkably accurate. The room mentioned more than any other was that where social gatherings took place. It was hung with either tapestries or paintings. At one side was a raised platform called an *estrado*, with hangings, floor covering, and sometimes a railing. Here sat the ladies usually on cushions, entertaining guests or doing needlework. Men occupied chairs near the dais. In winter the apartment was heated by perfumed char-

III

coal burning in one or more braziers. Lope de Vega and Calderón de la Barca among others spoke of the *estrado* (46). María de Zayas y Sotomayor wrote:

"At the head of the room was a rich *estrado*, with green velvet cushions excessively adorned with silver trimming and tassels, which competed with a beautiful little bed, forming at one side of the *estrado* a throne, seat, and shelter for lovely Lisis. . . The room was fenced in with many green velvet chairs and many little stools for the gentlemen to sit on so that they could enjoy the heat of a silver brazier which diffused perfume and warmed the platform from side to side" (47).

Alonso de Castillo Solórzano described a similar room. Hung with costly Flemish tapestries and Turkish rugs, it contained a large *estrado* with twenty-four red velvet cushions and two great silver braziers (48).

Authors of plays and tales listed sideboards of silver, cabinets, splendid secretaries (or *vargueños*), benches, embroidered chairs, little silver tables, trunks, and beds. Such luxurious objects belonged at this time to members of the middle class as well as to the nobility. Pedro Fernández Navarrete wrote bitterly that the houses which seventy years ago were thought good enough for a grandee are rejected by common people and that the wives of artisans have in their homes finer furniture and more costly *estrados* than those belonging to the titled nobility of a short time ago (49). He went on to say:

"The gilded ceilings, the fireplaces and columns of marble demand small rooms with exquisite appointments, with a great many secretaries (*vargueños*) which serve only for appearance or correspondence, many and varied small tables, some inlaid with different kinds of stones, others with silver, others with ebony, and ivory, and others of a thousand different kinds of wood brought from Asia. Flowers are thought to have no scent if their vases are clay, and so they are made of silver or more costly material. . . Neither are individuals content with the hangings which a few years before adorned the houses of princes. The taffetas and embossed leather of Spain, so famous in other places, are not good enough in this. The twill and tatters with which Spanish taste used to be content have been changed in favour of rich cloths of Milan and Florence, and expensive tapestries of Brussels. In rooms where there are no hangings are placed fine pictures, valued only for the fame of their artists and many of them with less modesty than is suitable in Christian homes" (50).

El día de fiesta by Juan de Zabaleta depicts the colourful interior of

FIGURE 40

INTERIOR
XVII century furniture
shown in a painting, *The
Vocation of Saint Matthew,*
by Juan de Pareja in the
Museo Nacional del Prado,
Madrid

another seventeenth-century house. A great unlighted silver brazier
surrounded by flowers in one of the rooms is likened to a fountain.
Another brazier with a case of ebony and ivory, set on a Tyrian rug
woven in a carnation pattern, seems a pool of hot ashes. Benches,
leather chairs with gilded nails, *vargueños* supporting statues, cabinets
of curios, tapestries, and crimson hangings impress the visitor with their
splendour (51).

A painting of the *Vocation of Saint Matthew* by Juan de Pareja
affords a glimpse into the seventeenth-century home of a citizen of
substance (Fig. 40). Here are seen pictures and draperies, a sideboard
made up of shelves bearing silver platters and urns, a sturdy wooden
table with low, box stretchers, covered with an Oriental rug, and a
rectangular side chair with leather back and seat attached by gilded
nails. Most interesting of all is an open *vargueño* standing in the background. The *vargueño* apparently did not always serve as a writing desk;
here it is a bookcase. In a story by Mariana de Caravajal y Saavedra
it became a treasure chest, guarding more than eight thousand ducats
worth of doubloons and jewels (52).

Vargueños have the simplicity, rigid rectangularity, and austere
dignity that have always appealed to Spanish taste in furniture. Their

FIGURE 41

VARGUEÑO
XVI-XVII century
vargueño in the City Art
Museum, St. Louis

construction is like the cabinet work of no other nation. Pleasing lines of French or Italian show pieces are missing, and crudities appear in even the best examples. What they lack in refinement is made up in strength, the thick slabs of walnut being firmly dovetailed and bound with more iron than necessary. Colour and boldness of design allow them to hold their own against the richest background. When open, the effect is one of flamboyant splendour, but even the most beautiful interiors, like Moorish *artesonados*, will not stand too close an examination if one is looking for perfection of detail. The rough method of pounding large hinge nails through the lid to the front is probably in agreement with a guild regulation demanding durability of construction. Three little shells placed over these nail ends are a concession to appearance made only on valuable pieces of furniture.

Anyone with a pretension to wealth must have owned a *vargueño* during the seventeenth century, as writing cabinets are mentioned so often in household inventories, and so many are still in existence. By this time the classic type, decorated inside with architectural motives and a mosaic of linked ivory plaques, led in popularity. The ivory plaques were usually faceted with black lines in rude imitation of jewels. Several *vargueños* of this type are in the collection of the Hispanic Society. Among the many others displayed in American collections are those at the City Art Museum in St. Louis (Fig. 41), Detroit Institute of Arts, and the Denver Art Museum (Fig. 42). On some *vargueño* drawers, crosses are inlaid under shell hoods, indicating church ownership, such as on cabinet S45 (Fig. 134). Often the ivory plaques are etched with formalized flower and scroll patterns and the faces of the drawers enlivened by touches of red or blue paint. An unusual and original *vargueño* (S77, Figs. 146 and 147) at the Hispanic Society, its stand matching the cabinet's interior, has plaques engraved with scrolled leafage, portrait heads, and animals of the chase like those on Talavera or Triana pottery of the seventeenth and eighteenth centuries. A form of *vargueño* lacking Arabic elements is shown in Figs. 43, 44. On the outside are vases of flowers, scrolls, and leafage, and inside curled leaves and rosettes without architectural framework. The table has an inlaid frieze which matches the cabinet. Inlaid work of this style, characteristic of Asturias, may be seen on the bench in Fig. 65.

A variation of the *vargueño* cabinet is the *papelera*, used as its name indicates, for storing papers. It is usually smaller than the former and lacks a writing lid. The absence of the drop lid makes this a colourful piece of furniture, since the gilded and painted drawers are never concealed. *Papeleras*, unlike *vargueños*, had feet. Those on *papelera* S50 (Fig. 149) at the Hispanic Society are pear shaped. They were supported by narrow tables such as the one (S27, Fig. 156) in the collection of the Society with turned and blocked legs and iron braces. A variety of

FIGURE 42

VARGUEÑO

XVII century *vargueño* in the Spanish Room of the Denver Art Museum

46

FIGURE 43

ASTURIAN
VARGUEÑO
XVII century inlaid cabinet
and table in the collection
of Don José Luis
Ferreiro, Cangas de Tineo
(Oviedo)

FIGURE 44

ASTURIAN
VARGUEÑO
The *vargueño* in Fig. 43,
shown with the lid open

47

seventeenth-century carved and inlaid *vargueños* and *papeleras* at the museum in the *Diputación*, Pontevedra, appear in Figs. 45, 46. The second from the right in Fig. 45 is nearly identical with S50.

Primitive tables of Gothic days, consisting of planks on crude trestles or central-footed posts, developed during the Renaissance into a new form built in vast numbers during the seventeenth century and still used all over the Peninsula. They ranged in length from little kitchen tables, now removed from their humble settings and used as coffee tables, to massive structures requiring several sets of legs. The tops, always plain, were supported by open lyre-scrolled trestles or splayed legs braced with decorative wrought iron. When straight legs were attached to the corners, they were usually joined by low box stretchers rendering iron braces unnecessary (Fig. 47). The method by which the tops and trestle legs were joined is uniquely Spanish. Across the width of the underside of the top a mortise was cut into which a crosspiece, made in two parts and joined by turn bolts, was fitted, finished at the table edge, and moulded. To the crosspiece the legs were either hinged or mortised and tenoned. Thus, like their Gothic antecedents, these tables were collapsible either by folding the legs or by removing the screws holding both parts of the crosspiece together.

An example of the table with open-scrolled lyre supports is illustrated in Fig. 49. Another is shown in a carved *Annunciation* exhibited at the Hispanic Society (D67). Although the relief is dated late seventeenth

FIGURE 45

INTERIOR
XVII century *vargueños*
and *papeleras* in the
Diputación, Pontevedra

century, the Virgin is seated in an early Renaissance hip-joint chair, indicating that old pieces of furniture continued to be used in spite of changing styles.

Turned, splayed legs as well as those of lyre-shape were made for tables throughout the Peninsula. Tables with drawers were upheld by either lyre or splayed trestles, or by fixed legs braced by box stretchers instead of ironwork. Drawers and friezes were carved with either geometric paneling or Renaissance leafage as bold and clear as if worked in metal. Below them appeared an outward-flared moulding, a feature essentially Spanish. Drawer pulls consisted of turned wooden knobs or iron drop handles. Sometimes tables had drawers at the back as well as the front, but usually the back frieze was fixed and as decorative as the face. Drawers were often separated by scrolled brackets (Fig. 48). At the Isabella Stewart Gardner Museum, Boston, is a table so long that it requires three pairs of supporting legs, with drawers carved with geometric patterns (Fig. 50).

A refectory table in the collection of William E. Boggs, New York, is supported by three sets of scrolled lyre-shaped trestles (Fig. 51). This seventeenth-century table was formerly in the palace of Don Ignacio Abadal of Barcelona. The six-legged table in Fig. 52 was photographed in the palace of Don Francisco Pendás Cortés in Labra.

Among paintings showing seventeenth-century interiors, a picture of the *Christ Child with the Crown of Thorns* by Zurbarán displays a table

FIGURE 46

INTERIOR
XVII century furniture in the Diputación, Pontevedra

FIGURE 47

TABLE
XVII century table
formerly in the collection
of Otto Bernheimer,
Munich

FIGURE 48

WALNUT TABLE
XVI-XVII century, 165 cm.
(65 inches) long, 82 cm.
(32 inches) deep, 89 cm.
(35 inches) high. In the
collection of William E.
Boggs, New York

FIGURE 49

TRESTLE TABLE
XVII century table with
lyre-shaped supports in the
Casa Saborit, Argentona

51

FIGURE 50

REFECTORY TABLE
XVII century oak table
315 cm. (10 feet, 4 inches)
long, 66 cm. (24 inches)
deep, 76 cm. (30 inches)
high. In the Isabella
Stewart Gardner Museum,
Boston

with drawers. It has turned and blocked legs, an undecorated frieze with knob drawer pulls, box stretchers, and a top with moulded edge.

Rich velvet or brocade table covers continued to be in style well into the seventeenth century according to interiors painted by Velázquez, one appearing in his portrait of Diego del Corral y Arellano.

The only early Spanish tables with round tops are said to be gate-leg tables (53). Sometimes instead of having extra supports to form the gate, two of the legs were split.

A kind of table belonging to Upper Aragón, but never widely used, was the Ligurian table, illustrated by Fig. 53. Copied from French and Italian models, it usually had an extension top resting on carved trestle ends joined by a horizontal stretcher fitted with turned or fluted balusters (54).

In Portugal, as well as Spain, lathe work became increasingly important, and Portuguese turners gained fame for their skill. Their favourite patterns were spiral and bulbous. Spiral turning was perhaps more popular for chair frames and bedposts, and bulbous turning for table legs. Ebony, which was imported in large quantities from India, was found desirable for elaborate lathe work because of its gleaming strength. Bulbous turning is illustrated in Fig. 54.

The simple, dignified monk's chair remained preëminently in use throughout this century and even to the end of the next. According to Asúa, in the seventeenth century it was the chair of private houses, convents, halls, barber shops, sacristies, and the platforms of schoolmasters and judges; it was the armchair of chapter houses and guard rooms (55). Sometimes its arms were wide, like those of Fig. 55, and then supported by curved or scrolled brackets. There are two theories explaining the extraordinary width of the arms of some chairs. One is that they were used to balance cups and dishes, taking the place of tables in religious houses, and the other that they supported large and weighty books when monks read and wrote (56). Both explanations seem logical, as furniture was scarce and books were heavy. It is practically impossible to distinguish early seventeenth-century *sillones fraileros* from those built near the end of the previous century, because styles changed slowly where communication was so difficult and because the durability of the earlier chairs allowed them to remain so long in use. *Sillones fraileros*, whether old or new, were standard properties in court paintings during this age of portraiture. A chair covered with red velvet appears in a portrayal of a Spanish lady (A92) dressed and rouged in the fashion of María Luisa of Orleans by an unknown court painter, at the Hispanic Society. Chairs of this type are constantly mentioned in contemporary inventories. An illustrative example (Fig. 56) exhibited in the winter of 1937–38 at the Burlington Fine Arts Club, London, is one of a pair owned by Don Pablo de Azcárate, then ambassador to England. The chair is walnut, upholstered in crimson velvet with gold tissue and red velvet *appliqué*. It has a fixed seat and appears lighter than early Renaissance chairs, but otherwise differs little from them.

An ingenious adaptation of the rectangular armchair is that in which sits Prince Alonso *el Caro*, son of Philip the Third (57). The chair (Fig. 57) has a velvet back, topped with ball finials and edged with wide fringe. Below the seat runs a balustrade with turned spindles giving an effect of lightness but, together with the bar between the arms, confining the child securely. The base is set upon spherical castors.

FIGURE 51

REFECTORY TABLE
XVII century walnut table 325 cm (10 feet, 8 inches) long, 95 cm (37 inches) deep, 84 cm (33 inches) high. Formerly in the palace of Don Ignacio Abadal, Barcelona; now in the collection of William E. Boggs, New York

FIGURE 52

REFECTORY TABLE
XVII century table in
Palace of Don Francisco
Pendás Cortés,
Labra (Oviedo)

Another interesting child's chair stands in the foreground of a portrait of Prince Philip Prosper, son of Philip the Fourth and Mariana of Austria. The Prince was born in 1657 and was painted by Velázquez possibly two years later. The little chair has the square, heavy lines of earlier pieces, but its arms are softened by padded red velvet, matching that of back and seat, attached by gilded nails and trimmed with gold braid. At the right, stands a square stool with baluster-turned legs, ball feet, box stretchers, and red velvet cushion embellished with gold braid and ornate gilt tassels. Such stools began to replace chests as seats along the walls of anterooms and passages and in drawing-rooms as described in writings of the time. Concerning the use of chairs and stools Julio Monreal stated:

"Cushions were only for ladies; men sat on chairs or stools, according to the rank they held, since the chair at this time and even previously was offered only to a person whom one wished to honour for his social position, giving him who was esteemed less, or with whom one was more intimate, a stool" (58).

This was further borne out by Calderón who wrote that on the first visit one was usually given the formal chair, later a stool, and then a footstool (59).

About the middle of the century, the legs and side stretchers of *sillones fraileros* became turned and blocked following the fashion of Louis-the-Thirteenth chairs to which the baluster was almost indispensable. In following the styles of Louis the Thirteenth and his son, the sobriety of the Spanish straight line was sacrificed. Arms as well as supports came to be shaped with ring, baluster, or spiral turnings. The front stretcher, now turned, was placed high and a recessed stretcher added to brace the ends. A chair of this kind with leather upholstery and scrolled, instead of turned, arms may be seen at the right in Fig. 45. Toward the end of the century when the style of the Grand Monarch of France had thoroughly impressed its influence upon the woodwork of Spain, chairs appeared with tall, upholstered backs, scrolled or turned legs, and elaborate, Italianate, serpentine stretchers. Caning, said to have been taken from Oriental sources by the Portuguese and thence introduced into Europe, was a favourite covering for the late seventeenth-century, tall-backed chair which usually had a heavily carved crest and central splat (60). Its use was popular in those parts of the Peninsula where the climate was hot. At the end of the century, the

FIGURE 53

LIGURIAN TABLE
XVII century Aragonese table in a private collection in Fanlo (Huesca)

55

variety of chairs was great but their inspiration foreign. Because of their cost, French, Italian, and English types were used only in palaces or in homes of extremely wealthy persons.

A chair, attributed to the Portuguese, evolved naturally from the Renaissance armchair and became highly esteemed in Spain and the Catholic Netherlands. The furniture of Spaniards and Portuguese, a kindred people, was similar. Portugal was, in fact, a reluctant part of Spain from its annexation by Philip the Second in 1581 until the successful culmination of the revolution for independence in 1668. Oriental features such as caning, the Chinese cabriole leg, and use of lacquer were, perhaps, introduced to Europe by the Portuguese through their maritime trade with the East. Spiral turning is sometimes added to this list. Its vogue in Portugal was early, widespread, and intense, but historical proof of its origin and the reason for its sudden revival and development during the seventeenth century is lacking (61). Spaniards were not slow in adopting and developing Portuguese innovations. The seventeenth-century Portuguese chair had a tall back, arched at the crest and usually shaped at the base, topped with two or three pointed metal finials. It was upholstered with embossed leather stretched across the back and seat and fastened to back posts and seat rails by large

FIGURE 54

PORTUGUESE TABLE
XVII century table,
formerly in the
Kunstgewerbe Museum,
Düsseldorf

bosses. Seats were broad at the front, tapering somewhat toward the back. Legs, side and back stretchers were turned and blocked, and the feet, either ball-shaped or fluted and scrolled underneath in a form now called the Spanish foot, shown in Fig. 59. The wide, front stretcher, arched like the back cresting, was often in the shape of a rising, interlaced scroll. The arms were apt to be smooth, deeply scrolled, and rolled over at the ends such as those in Fig. 58. Leather upholstery for these chairs was adorned with coats of arms and embossed designs in the Renaissance taste. In Spain, Córdoba was the natural centre for manufacturing leather-covered chairs. Pérez Bueno stated that, because of their excellence, many were exported from Spain to France (62). English chairs were influenced by those of Portugal. Among the new features of the Orange-Stuart chairs, which entered England by way of Holland, were the Spanish foot, spiral and bulbous turnings, hoop-back cresting, and arch-scrolled front stretchers. Leather upholstery attached by large nails was never so popular in other countries as on the Peninsula.

According to a list of prices and wages compiled in 1680 at Segovia, leather-seated chairs were given as products of the cabinetmaker or

FIGURE 55

ARMCHAIR (*left*)
XVII century monk's chair in a private collection in Barcelona

FIGURE 56

ARMCHAIR (*right*)
XVII century chair in the collection of Don Pablo de Azcárate

57

FIGURE 57

CHILD'S CHAIR
XVII century armchair
shown in the painting
*Alonso el Caro, Son of
Philip the Third of Spain,*
attributed to Bartolomé
González

carver. When lathe work was desired for their decoration, the cabinet-maker assembled the framework in blank form and had it finished by the turner. A walnut armchair with back and seat of Eastern leather, fastened with gilded nails, was valued at fifty-eight *reales;* a high stool of the same style at thirty-three. Among other furniture than chairs listed under cabinetmaking were tables with iron braces, benches with or without hinged backs, footstools, beds, and brazier cases. A journey-man of the cabinetmakers' guild received six and a half *reales* a day, a journeyman of turnery three *reales,* and a master carpenter six *reales* (63). Carpenters living in cities now made little furniture other than plain chests of pine, workbenches, and beds to be covered by tex-tiles.

From the time of the late Renaissance onward, in country districts, humble carpenters made chairs, tables, and chests of elemental form with carvings often crude but fresh and original. Regional work differs slightly in the various districts of Spain. Carving was either geometric or floral, or consisted of simple gouge or chisel cuts arranged in unpretentious but striking patterns. Traditional designs were maintained, the rosette and wheel of Romanesque times being especially popular. In general, the all-wood chair was made in the north from native woods, and the rush-seated or corded chair in the east, south, and in the islands. Byne and Stapley stated that all-wood chairs with little arcades across their backs supported on turned spindles were from Aragón and Navarra, while both all-wood and corded chairs were from the province of Santander, known in Spain as *La Montaña*. According to these authors, in Castilla, Andalucía, and Cataluña the rush seat predominated and in

FIGURE 58

PORTUGUESE ARMCHAIR (*left*) XVII century leather-covered chair, formerly in the Kunstgewerbe Museum, Dresden

FIGURE 59

PORTUGUESE SIDE CHAIR (*right*) XVII century leather-covered chair in the Instituto de Valencia de Don Juan, Madrid

59

Mallorca, seats corded with ingenious patterns were more usual (64). The *Museo de Artes Decorativas* at Madrid possesses a large and interesting collection of regional chairs, several of which are nearly identical with those at the Hispanic Society. Three beautiful chairs in the former museum, probably from the province of Santander, are illustrated in Figs. 60–62. The first, one of a pair, shows a balustrade below the seat as well as across the back. Its hoop cresting is carved with rosettes and two snakes drinking from a chalice. The snake motive is carried out in undulating chisel cuts on the front legs. The second is an armchair with corded seat, which is an adaptation by a provincial carpenter of the elaborate late seventeenth-century palace chair. Its back has a central splat pierced to represent a vase of flowers, the cresting is shaped as a coronet flanked by scrolls below which stands the Hapsburg double-headed eagle. Chip carving ornaments practically every available surface including that of the unusual, outward-scrolled arms. The third

FIGURE 60

PROVINCIAL CHAIR
(*left*)
XVII century side chair in the Museo Nacional de Artes Decorativas, Madrid

FIGURE 61

PROVINCIAL
ARMCHAIR (*right*)
XVII century armchair with corded seat in the Museo Nacional de Artes Decorativas, Madrid

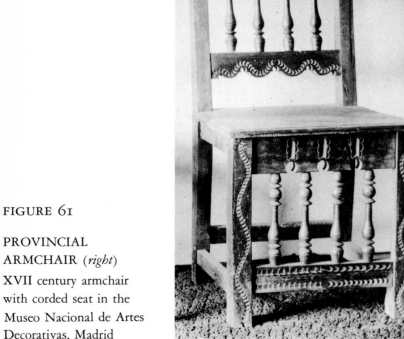

60

FIGURE 62

PROVINCIAL CHAIR (*left*) XVII century ladder back side chair in the Museo Nacional de Artes Decorativas, Madrid

FIGURE 63

PROVINCIAL CHAIR (*right*) XVII century chair with corded rope seat in the Minneapolis Institute of Arts

chair, a delicate and finely constructed example of regional work, has a wooden seat and turned and blocked supports. Its ladder back is carved with addorsed C-scrolls like those decorating the headpieces of many Portuguese beds. A small chair (Fig. 63) at The Minneapolis Institute of Arts is one of two said to have come from Santander. The seat of this chair is made of rope, corded in a diamond pattern. It has flat splats instead of spindles. The crosspiece at the top is pierced in the popular wheel design. The flat surfaces of the chair are lightly scored with chisel marks. Chairs were made of unequal height in the provinces of Andalucía, Murcia, and Valencia; the highest were reserved for men and placed at one side of the room (65). It was customary for the civic and religious dignitaries of a town to use all-wood chairs, usually walnut, made in the shape of *sillones fraileros*, their wooden backs carved with large coats of arms.

Low straight chairs usually with baluster backs, turned supports, and rush seats, in the style of seventeenth-century models, are still made in Spain and used in cottages, inns, and country churches. At Cáceres

FIGURE 64

FOLDING BENCH
XVII century bench with
the arms of Castile and
Charles V. 262 cm. (8 feet,
7 inches) long. Sold (to an
unknown buyer) at Parke-
Bernet Galleries in 1943

they are sold on Monday mornings below the *Plaza de la Constitución*, while in other places, they are piled on backs of donkeys and sold from door to door.

The Renaissance bench usually had leather or textile upholstery. It might also be plain with a central, metal plaque or carved escutcheon. Benches were used in mansions, public buildings, and churches during the seventeenth century. Church benches were placed in the sacristy or in private chapels, but later, in the next century, they were often arranged in parallel lines in the nave (66). Bench legs, like table legs, were either splayed and turned or shaped as lyres, their braces made of gracefully scrolled wrought iron. Many benches had hinges to fold the back such as the long armorial bench depicted in Fig. 64. Other examples of the all-wood bench include two at The Isabella Stewart Gardner Museum and another at the Fine Arts Gallery, San Diego. The bench with a central metal plaque is represented by S3 (Fig. 181) in the Society's collection. Around the back runs a border of rosettes made with a chisel.

Regional benches are closely akin to regional chairs, having backs carved with naturalistic motives or arcaded and set on spindles. At the Convent of *San Pelayo* are a number of inlaid and arcaded benches with wooden seat braces instead of ironwork (Fig. 65). The frame of a bench

(S1, Fig. 182) at the Hispanic Society is similar, but its spindles are missing and the seat is not original. The design along the back is identical with that of numerous pieces of furniture at Oviedo and a bench at the Palace of Ferrara, Avila. Without doubt, the Society's bench may be attributed to the same province. A small chestnut bench (S2, Fig. 183) in the collection of the Society probably comes from northern Spain where that wood was plentiful. Its forceful designs are in close accord with those which decorate northern, country-made chests of the same period. A strongly chiseled Castilian bench appears in Fig. 66.

Carving on regional chests is distinguished by its simplicity, vigour, and boldness. The treatment, consisting mainly of deep chisel cuts, is broad with little detail. The finest chests of this kind come from the north of Spain, those of Vizcaya and Asturias being particularly handsome. The lids are customarily plain and inside there are often small compartments for special objects. A chest (Fig. 67), its rosettes simplified and arranged geometrically, shows how the end stiles were sometimes lengthened to form feet. This method of construction is peculiarly Asturian (67). The end stiles are prolonged on a chest (Fig.

FIGURE 65

ASTURIAN BENCH
XVII century inlaid bench in the Convent of San Pelayo, Oviedo

FIGURE 66

CASTILIAN BENCH
XVII century carved bench
in the Museo Nacional de
Artes Decorativas, Madrid

68) at Vigo, which has leafy borders of chip carving, geometric panels, and rosettes. Although the decoration is simple, its effect is one of brilliance and richness, as is the carving on a chest (Fig. 69) which two women are using as a table for their chocolate cups. A chest (Fig. 70) called Navarrese, at the *Museo de Artes Decorativas*, Madrid, features the same kind of geometric Muhammadan paneling of incised lozenges in rectangular spaces, which occurs on the bases of *vargueños* and the backs of stretchers of many popular chairs. Repetition of geometric motives, reminiscent of Moorish design, indicates how slowly traditions

FIGURE 67

PROVINCIAL CHEST
XVII century carved chest
in the collection of Don
José Varela de Limia y
Menéndez, Noya (Coruña)

64

FIGURE 68

CARVED CHEST

XVII century chest in the
collection of Don Xavier
Ozores, Vigo

65

FIGURE 69

PROVINCIAL CHEST
XVII century carved chest
in Casa Condarco, San
Andrés de Valdebárzana
(Oviedo)

FIGURE 70

NAVARRESE CHEST
XVII century carved chest
in the Museo Nacional de
Artes Decorativas, Madrid

66

in woodwork passed on the Peninsula. A chest of the type executed in the Levantine region of Cataluña and Valencia, principally at Gerona where many are still to be seen, and in the Balearic Islands is pictured in Fig. 71. Such pieces, their design influenced by Italian work, were more ambitious examples than other country chests. They were usually decorated with applied blind arches, appearing not only on the exterior but on the inner side of the lid as well, and by out-jutting scrolled brackets and carved feet. In spite of a profusion of carved rosettes and leafage, the openings of the arches, usually left smooth, formed a dignified and pleasing composition. Like Gothic-Catalan chests, these are called either brides' or grooms' chests depending on whether or not the front opens to disclose drawers. Two Catalan grooms' chests (Fig. 71) belonging to John Nicholas Brown, Esquire, are on loan at the Rhode Island School of Design. The brackets and blind arches are applied with glue, but the rest of the carving is cut on the surface of the panels. The lids are decorated only on the underside, and the chest interiors lack the inner lids which originally were supplied.

FIGURE 71

CATALAN CHEST

XVII century groom's chest in the Rhode Island School of Design, Providence

67

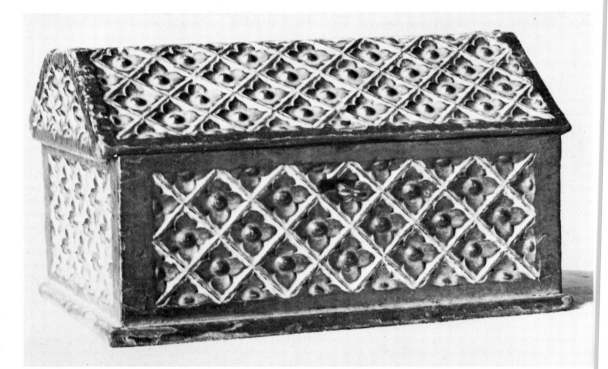

FIGURE 72

COFFRET

XVII century wooden reliquary box, painted and gilt. 16 × 27 cm. (6¼ × 10½ inches). In the Museo Episcopal, Vich

FIGURE 73

COFFRET

XVI century small wooden box ornamented with wrought iron. In the Museo Episcopal, Vich

For people of little means, plain wooden boxes were made to contain their belongings. One at the Hispanic Society (S57, Fig. 185) is distinguished for its stout construction and impressive ironwork. Chests with arched lids, covered with metal-studded cloth or leather, were the storage trunks of rich persons. In the seventeenth and eighteenth centuries they were often provided with gilded and carved trestle stands or feet. Typical of such trunks is one in a private collection at Barcelona (Fig. 76). Covered with velvet fastened with brass nail heads and double-headed eagle mounts, it has gilded paw feet. One chest (S59, Fig. 184) at the Hispanic Society belongs to this class. The brass mounts, as is often the case on velvet-covered chests, are pierced with delicate scrolls. Its lid is only slightly rounded. Leather was equally popular with velvet as upholstery for trunks. That which protects a chest with gilded metal work and paw feet at the Rhode Island School of Design is plain beneath its brass studs, while that covering a coffer (Fig. 77) owned by Señor Don Carlos de la Concha, Villaviciosa, Oviedo, is chiseled with a profusion of detail, consequently lacking any metal work except its lock plate.

Small table boxes of wood or metal, aping every style of chest, were made from Gothic times through the seventeenth century (Figs. 72–75). They were often mentioned by seventeenth-century writers as used for jewel or trinket cases, and boxes for game pieces or for sewing materials. Another use is given in *La buena guarda* by Lope de Vega. The sacristan said that when ladies went to Mass, wrapped in embroidered mantles over delicate cambric and resembling cranes because of the height of their clogs, they sat down upon an *estrado* with cushions and asked politely for their beauty boxes. These, when open, revealed a confusion of more colours than an artist's palette and enough jars to mystify an apothecary (68). At the Hispanic Society there are two table boxes. One (S49, Fig. 186) is especially designed and constructed as an apothecary's cabinet with inscribed drawers containing wells to hold uncut stones and racks to support mortars for grinding stones into powders. The box, in poor repair and once painted with brilliant colours, has a hinged fall front with a coat of arms. The other table box (S54, Fig. 188) at the Society, veneered with chevrons of yellow barberry and reddish arbutus or briar, has a velvet-lined compartment and drawer for trinkets. This small, rather plain box illustrates in a simple way a different technique in the decoration of furniture; the revival of the old art of marquetry.

During the Gothic and Renaissance periods, ivory, mother-of-pearl, metal, exotic woods, and semiprecious stones were inlaid into a ground of solid wood cut out to receive each tiny piece, but during the seventeenth century both pattern and ground were laid down as a veneer on a matrix of glue, a process now termed marquetry. Since the veneer on chest S54 is not pictorial, as is usual in the case of marquetry, it may be more correctly described as parquetry, a veneer made by joining together vari-coloured geometric pieces. Marquetry was an improved method for building up elaborate patterns in rare, imported woods, many of which were not suitable for constructing the entire carcass of a large piece of furniture. Ebony from India because of its intense dark colour, strength, and gloss was a favourite wood for veneers, especially when dramatically combined with ivory, tortoise shell, or metal. During this century, ebony and shell cabinets with gilt-bronze mounts, architecturally treated, with matching stands, were extremely well liked in Italy, Flanders, Germany, and France. The cabinetmakers of the Low Countries were so skilled at this work that Henry the Fourth of France sent French workmen to learn their secrets (69). Some Flemish cabinets had paintings on glass, copper, or enamels. Many magnificent German cabinets were little worlds in themselves, fitted with all kinds of implements ingeniously concealed and decorated with classical allusions and allegories (70). So many miniature edifices were imported into Spain from Nuremburg that they had to be prohibited by Philip the Third in 1603 in order to protect the home industry. They must have been copied on the Peninsula to a great extent at the end of the sixteenth century, since Pedro Gutiérrez, tapestry maker to Queen Isabella, found it necessary on behalf of cabinetmakers to present a memorial to the King, saying that cabinets and secretaries which were worth from five hundred to seven hundred *reales* when bought from Germany were now made in Spain for two hundred and fifty and three hundred *reales* (71). Ebony and ivory cabinets of this type were often spoken of by Spanish authors, such as Carduchi and Alonso de Castillo, and were entered in many contemporary inventories (72). An inventory of the Duke of Lerma's goods printed in 1622 lists as many as eighteen secretaries and a bookcase from Germany described as made of black mulberry wood. Ebony objects, contained among the Duke's many magnificent beds, trunks, tables, and over a hundred chairs and stools of embroidered velvet or leather, were three bronze-trimmed clocks and eight mirror frames (73). Cabinets were not only popular in Spain but also in her colonies. A book describing the religious art of Santa Fé de Bogotá

FIGURE 74

GOTHIC COFFRET
XV-XVI century wooden
box with traces of gilt and
gesso. In the Instituto de
Valencia de Don Juan,
Madrid

FIGURE 75

COFFRET

XVII century reliquary box
of carved gilt wood, dated
1655. 15 × 24 cm.
(5⅞ × 9½ inches). In the
Museo Episcopal, Vich

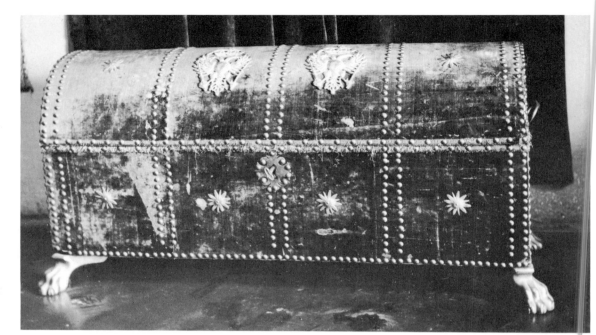

FIGURE 76

VELVET-COVERED
CHEST

XVII century trunk on feet
in a private collection in
Barcelona

states that from 1650 to 1690 there worked in that city, then the capital
of the Spanish viceroyalty of New Granada, Miguel de Acuña, ingenious
cabinetmaker and worker in veneer. He made with taste and mastery,
a great quantity of frames, secretaries (*vargueños*), chests, and furniture
of ebony, walnut, and other fine woods. Among the objects he built were
secretaries filled with drawers, with delicate balusters, veneered with
tortoise shell and ivory plaques on which were engraved black, grotesque
animals, hunting scenes, and flowers and leaves whimsically combined (74).

FIGURE 77

CHEST

XVII century leather-
covered trunk in the
collection of Don Carlos
de la Concha, Villaviciosa

A striking example of the Spaniard's conception of the Italianate architectural cabinet (Fig. 78) is a massive piece without a stand, belonging to Señor Don Eduardo Dibós Dammert of Peru, exhibited for many years at The Brooklyn Museum. It is decorated with tortoise shell, mother-of-pearl, and religious pictures painted at the time of Murillo. It is a replica of the Monastery of *San Francisco*, Lima, Peru, and, according to a plaque attached to its base, was made at Sevilla in 1657 by Juan de Espinosa. A less exotic cabinet is illustrated in Fig. 79.

A tall, three-storied, inlaid cabinet consisting of a desk between two cupboards was occasionally built in Spain during the seventeenth century. The spindled top story formed a ventilated food cupboard (*fresquera*) for fruit, cheese, and bread. Similar inclosed shelves are sometimes hung on the walls of Spanish dining rooms. A niche of tile (Fig. 49) built into the wall above the *lavabo* was a usual place to display dishes in the dining room. Tall cupboards in one or more stories were used more often in church sacristies and public buildings than in domestic interiors. Many of those now standing in Spanish homes were taken from these earlier settings. It was customary for such pieces of furniture to follow the lead of architecture and consequently many had pediments in the late Herreran style and small, Moorish-type, geometric door panels carved with leafage and set off by heavy mouldings. At the Town Hall, Bayona (Pontevedra), there is a painted and carved cupboard or wardrobe (Fig. 80) built in 1679. Its paneled doors bear the arms of Castilla and León and the emblems of the town. Along the stiles run linked oval and square medallions like those seen on *vargueño* stands, and on monks' chairs. The cabinet is supported by a plinth with bracket feet.

A view of the dining room in the home of Don Luis Suárez-Infiesta at Gijón shows another tall cupboard (Fig. 81) which has a spindled upper story. The panels of its doors are carved with large floral ornaments. A number of pieces of furniture in this room belong to the seventeenth century: a centre table with spool-turned legs and inlaid frieze, leather-seated chairs, and a Catalan chest used as a sideboard. Another tall cupboard appears, together with a Basque kneading trough and settle, in the provincial kitchen depicted in Fig. 82.

During the seventeenth century, beds of state, their woodwork concealed beneath sumptuous coverings, continued to be used. At the same time, an innovation appeared in the treatment of bed frames which, from this century on, received more attention, draperies consequently

FIGURE 78

SEVILLIAN CABINET
Three views (*side views at top of opposite page*) of an elaborate cabinet built in 1657 at Sevilla by Juan de Espinosa. Approximately 137 cm (54 inches) high, 88 cm (34½ inches) wide, 43 cm (17 inches) deep. In the collection of Don Eduardo Dibós Dammert, Lima, Peru

74

FIGURE 78

SIDE VIEW (*left*)

FIGURE 78

DETAIL
OF SIDE (*right*)
A closer view of the
paintings on the cabinet

becoming fewer and the general appearance lighter and more modern. The beds at El Pazo de Villar de Ferreiros (Galicia), for example, were hung with galloon-trimmed, vari-coloured curtains, but the frame of one is said to be turned walnut. Another is of painted wood crowned by a bronze image of the Virgin, flanked by angels of the same metal, and a third has a frame of rosewood, probably never hidden because of its beauty and value (75).

In Spain, during this century, bed structure developed into three types: those with architectural headpieces in the Herreran style decorated with metal mounts and turned posts topped with pointed finials, Portuguese-type beds elaborately turned with spiral twists and flamelike finials, and those having headboards shaped with baroque scrolls and hung separately to the wall. The Herreran bed has been attributed to the region of Castilla, and the Portuguese and baroque types to Cataluña and the Balearic Islands (76). The baroque silhouette (Fig. 83), a later development, belongs rather to the beds of the eighteenth century, as it did not reach the height of its vogue until then. An Herreran bed hung with pointed red silk damask trimmed with tassels and gold galloon may be seen in Fig. 84. The dark wood of its pedimented headpiece is brightened by mountings of pierced brass terminating in a brass figure of the Virgin and Child. It is built up of four orders of balusters and somewhat resembles a *reja* grill. The turnings of the brass-trimmed posts, spindles, and finials feature large circular disks. Ball feet uphold the bed. A turned bed at the Buffalo Historical Society is representative of the

FIGURE 79

INLAID CABINET
XVII century cabinet in
the Victoria and Albert
Museum, London

FIGURE 80

WARDROBE
Painted and carved
cupboard or wardrobe built
in 1679. In the Town Hall,
Bayona

77

FIGURE 81

DINING ROOM

XVII century furniture including a tall cupboard (*left*) in the home of Don Luis Suárez-Infiesta at Gijón (Oviedo)

Portuguese form. Its posts and the balusters of the back are turned in ring, spiral, and bulbous shapes. The crested headpiece, closely carved with rising scrolls, two terminating in birds' heads, recalls East Indian work. The Historical Society also possesses a rose-coloured brocade valance which belongs to the bed, its points edged with cream fringe and separated by tassels of the same shade. The elaboration with which posts, balusters, and headpieces of Portuguese-type beds are twisted and scrolled is shown in Fig. 85.

A conclusion drawn from the Segovian price list of 1680 is that plain bed frames were made by carpenters, turned bedposts and balusters by turners, and elaborate beds decorated with painting, carving, turning, or metal work were assembled by cabinetmakers. Turners charged sixteen *reales* for their work on a walnut bed with posts, balusters, and finials, but cabinetmakers received at least a hundred and forty *reales* for assembling a bed of this kind. When not making posts for furniture, turners produced wheels, ninepins, chessmen, checkers, spinning wheels, chocolate mills, reels, lace bobbins, and handles for all sorts of tools (77).

A piece of furniture particularly Spanish is the brazier, a heating device which is still used, mainly in country inns and cottages, all over the

78

FIGURE 82

KITCHEN WITH BASQUE CUPBOARD
XVII century Basque cupboard, settle and kneading trough shown at the Exposición Ibero-Americano 1929-1930 at Sevilla

Peninsula. Its ancient origin is shown by the number of decorative Roman examples that persist. Gothic braziers which have been preserved, are made of iron or stone with simple architectural decoration.

After the influx of precious metals from the Indies during the Renaissance, massive silver and even gold braziers appeared designed in the plateresque style. In spite of regulations by Philip the Second and his son forbidding the use of silver (78), inventories and seventeenth-century novels continued to mention silver braziers as common pieces of furniture in wealthy households (79). Their use spread from Spain to the Low Countries and France, thence to the bedrooms and dressing rooms of English mansions. In 1689 Louis the Fourteenth owned eight silver examples, five of which were described as *braziers d'argent d'Espagne*. Their production and sale was suppressed in France during the same year to protect the use of silver for currency (80). The fire basins of Spanish braziers, usually round in shape and made of copper, were set in wood, metal, or porcelain stands of one or two stories, decorated in the current fashion. Some seventeenth-century stands were built of ebony inlaid with ivory and fenced in with balusters. A brazier at the Buffalo Historical Society represents perhaps the most popular type in

79

FIGURE 83

BAROQUE
HEADBOARD

Scrolled and painted
headboard, 155 cm.
(61 inches) high, for an
XVIII century bed in the
Museo Episcopal, Vich

common use. With turned ball feet the heavy, flat wooden platform studded with brass nail heads is raised to a comfortable height. Foot braziers and those having frames decorated with balusters and sheathed in brass are listed under cabinetmaking in the Segovian price list of 1680, valued from forty-four to fifty-five *reales* (81).

Another seventeenth-century type, covered with a wire cage, in a house at Montehermoso (Cáceres) appears in Fig. 86. The framework has four holes into which a table with turned legs is set. When the brazier is lighted, the table's red woolen, embroidered cover is exchanged for a long skirt in which slits are cut to accommodate the legs and feet.

A brazier (S79, Fig. 189) at the Hispanic Society has a top story

80

FIGURE 84

HERRERAN BED
XVII century bed hung
with pointed red silk
damask in the Montenegro
Collection, Lugo

FIGURE 85

PORTUGUESE BED
XVII century bed with
turned posts in the Vic-
toria and Albert Museum,
London

82

with a pan to warm the hands. Its columnar legs are fluted and gilded and its scalloped platforms covered with gleaming brass foil attached by many nails. According to an inscription around the top, the piece was made in 1641 at Zaragoza for the Count of Robles. It bears the arms of Castilla, Castilla and León, Navarra, France, and those of Robles charged with a cross. Fuel for Spanish braziers usually consisted of charcoal in a bed of olive-stone ash. Breton de la Martinière, writing about braziers in the nineteenth century, said that in accord with the Spanish fondness for perfume, powdered sandalwood and other fragrant woods were placed on the fire (82). Perfuming the fuel of braziers must have been a common custom as Manuel Bretón de los Herreros, famous dramatist of the same century, said,

> Sometimes the solid charcoal smokes,
> The rising cloud of vapour chokes,
> But—
> None will heed the vapours dire
> If lavender's placed upon the fire
> In the brazier (83).

In the *Diario* of Madrid, September 5th, 1795, Mexican perfumed tablets fragrant enough to last all day were advertised (84). Breton de la Martinière wrote that when the charcoal was improperly lighted, it used up the oxygen of the room and exuded a dangerous gas affecting first the children who were nearer the floor. He stated that in some places, especially Cataluña, coal dust, also dangerous, was substituted for charcoal, but assured us that crushed olive stones, the fuel of Valencia and other parts where olives were plentiful, were efficient and safe. Their unpleasant odor was claimed to be corrected in most homes by tobacco smoke (85).

Braziers are prepared for the day, out-of-doors, so that the obnoxious gas from freshly lighted coals will escape into the air. A woman performing this task at Valladolid is seen in Fig. 87. At one side is the tube or chimney which she uses to draw the fire until it is well lighted, and in her hands are a fan and a stirrer. It requires considerable skill to produce an evenly burning fire. She is using charcoal of pine and is banking it with ashes to preserve its heat and check the consumption of fuel. It was customary to place the brazier in the middle of the room. Nineteenth-century authors feared that its traditional use would be ousted by the increasing installation of French and English chimney pieces (86).

FIGURE 86

INTERIOR
WITH BRAZIER

XVII century type of table
brazier with a wire cage in
a house at Montehermoso
(Cáceres)

A verse or two from Bretón de los Herreros' long poem will show how close the brazier was to the hearts of the Spanish people.

> I have no chef to cook my feast
> Nor set the table of a priest
> But—
> Take my food with joy profound
> From the shelf that circles round
> The brazier.
>
> The wide-flung chimney piece I know
> Puts forth a greater roar and show
> But—
> Draw up close, for never fear
> You'll hear more tales, more secrets dear
> By the brazier (87).

Lady Tenison wrote in further praise: "Give me the Spanish 'brasero', pure and primitive type! with its simple circular stand, its white ashes, its red-hot charcoal, its exciting shovel, and its protecting wire-work

FIGURE 87

BRAZIER
Woman preparing a
modern brazier pan at
Valladolid using a chimney,
fan and stirrer

cover; give me its gentle, tranquil heat, the centre towards which so-
ciability converges, its circular accompaniment of joyous faces. Give me
the mutual confidence which its mild warmth imparts, the equality
with which this is distributed; and if, between two lights, give me the
tranquil brilliancy diffused by its bright-red coals, softly reflecting the
fire of two Arab eyes, the transparency of an oriental skin" (88).

FIGURE 88

CONSOLE
AND MIRROR
XVIII century furniture in
the palace of the Duke of
Alba, Sevilla

86

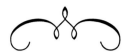

THE EIGHTEENTH CENTURY

IV

SPAIN in the eighteenth century made an exceptional but brief recovery from the decadent period suffered during late Hapsburg rule. Governed by Bourbons, the country attempted to come abreast the advanced civilization of other European nations. French influence predominated as soon as Philip the Fifth, grandson of the king of France, claimed the throne. Enlightenment and reform mainly benefited the higher classes whose ranks included many foreigners, while the common people clung to old ideas and ways of living.

Magnificent and formal furniture by André Charles Boulle and other famous artist-craftsmen under Louis the Fourteenth was copied in Spain at the beginning of the century. However, the gayer, more intimate style, for convenience termed Louis the Fifteenth, ruled Spanish cabinetmaking. Its early rococo phase, with designs featuring such rustic ornaments as rocks, shells, and foliage, became as popular at the Spanish court as at Paris. In construction, its chief characteristic was the curved line. On all kinds of furniture, cabriole legs of graceful contour took the place of straight ones. Objects were small, fragile, and light in colour. Comfort, detail, and workmanship were of the greatest importance. Superb ormolu mounts and porcelain plaques, made in Spain at Alcora or Buen Retiro, added a final touch of luxury. Mosaic or pictorial veneers in mahogany, rosewood, tulipwood, and other rare varieties were greatly admired. Panels of Eastern lacquer were also highly prized as the vogue for Oriental art objects, which started in the seventeenth century, continued during a good part of the eighteenth. White or pastel shades of lacquer, or paint, and gilding decorated seats and beds. Foreign furnishings were available as models when the example set by Philip the Fifth, who imported furniture from his homeland, was followed by wealthy Spaniards who traveled or studied in France. Copies of French pieces were executed for important personages, sometimes faultlessly, but usually with less nicety of craftsmanship, spoiling the purity of the design but with enough exaggeration to add warmth and richness.

The exuberance of the rococo style is pictured by a marble-topped console and matching mirror (Fig. 88) in the Sevillian palace of the Duke of Alba. Carved mirrors and consoles formed important additions to fine eighteenth-century interiors, in agreement with the French desire for brighter, more elegant rooms. Small mirrors with heavy, asymmetrical frames were also used for wall decoration, as were sconces, called cornucopias because their rococo frames somewhat resembled horns of plenty. Rooms of state had huge sheets of mirror glass edged with borders of gilded wood or metal set into the wall. So popular were mirrors that Philip the Fifth in 1736 established a royal factory for making them at San Ildefonso (89). The looking-glasses, which came to be the largest made anywhere, were designed principally for royal palaces or to be used as royal presents. Some, with their frames, weighed as much as nine tons (90).

That the Duke of Alba's console with mirror is an early piece is proclaimed by its serpentine stretcher and four caryatid supports, French motives of the previous century. Later, consoles were fastened to the wall at the back and upheld at the front by two S-shaped, inward-scrolled legs. Marble of the richest grain was sought for the tops of such tables. The over-elaborate and top-heavy pediment of the mirror and the bulging scrolls of the table supports were features which had greater appeal to the Spanish than to the French.

Although furniture became more diversified in type during the eighteenth century, few new objects were designed. In the most fashionable city mansions, all varieties of occasional and gaming tables appeared, lighter in frame than their predecessors and curved in outline. Commodes, small desks, and chests of drawers were copied from the French, but they never completely took the place of the traditional chest raised on a stand and decked with coverings and metal work in the current mode. The day bed, so well liked in France, was less used on the Peninsula. The settee, however, gained in popularity. One (Fig. 89) in the Convent of *San Pelayo* at Oviedo, with gilded frame and upholstery of red silk damask trimmed with red silk galloon and fringe, reveals the new trend in taste. Its back and arms are still square; serpentine stretchers continue to be used, and the upholstery is tacked on with nails in the old way. The arms are upheld by scrolled supports and set back, leaving the front of the seat free to allow room for the panniers which

88

FIGURE 89

SETTEE

XVIII century seat upholstered in red silk damask, in the Convent of San Pelayo, Oviedo

were then in fashion for ladies' skirts. The cabriole legs are in the new style but are of ungainly contour, projecting awkwardly beyond the seat. Carved scrolls edging the seat apron are broken and eccentric, lacking the fluidity of French scrolling. Whatever technical faults this seat may show in comparison with pieces in the Gallic taste, it is undeniably picturesque and vivacious in colour.

The interpretation of French rococo by a Spanish workman is shown by a side chair (Fig. 90) at the Philadelphia Museum. Although it has a curved back, the chair is reminiscent of the so-called Portuguese chairs made in the previous century. The rear legs, turned instead of curved, continue above the seat to raise the back higher than was recommended by Frenchmen whose concern about possible damage to the elaborate powdered coiffures of the time caused the low back to flourish. Turned stretchers and a central piece with rising arch, similarly shaped to the front stretchers of earlier times, brace the cabriole legs. French cabrioles, after a transitional phase, were constructed with such perfect balance that they could uphold the lightened chair frames without the use of stretchers. Cockleshells and other carved decorations on the Philadelphia chair remind one of early metal bosses and fail to blend harmoniously into the design. The leather upholstery, although French in pattern, is a feature typically Spanish. Other European nations at this time favoured softer fabrics, figured silks or tapestries, and the craft of decorating leather consequently declined.

89

FIGURE 90

SIDE CHAIR (*left*)
XVIII century chair with
leather upholstery in the
Philadelphia
Museum of Art

FIGURE 91

SIDE CHAIR (*right*)
XVIII century lacquered
chair in the Museo
Arqueológico Nacional,
Madrid

Leather upholstery attached by nails is also used for an eighteenth-century armchair (S12, Fig. 198) at the Hispanic Society. The back of this chair is tall and rectangular like those made in France during the reign of the Sun King. Its seat is square, and its scrolled arms are set directly over the front supports, but the chair displays the new lightness in construction which came in with the eighteenth century. Its scrolled legs are without stretchers, and the underframing of the seat is gracefully curved. Spanish rococo furniture can usually be detected from French by its prodigal use of wood, old structural methods, or the introduction of traditional Spanish details into the carving or metal work.

England contributed the second most important foreign influence over Spanish furniture design and decoration during this century, in spite of intermittent wars over the control of Spain's great colonial empire. Queen-Anne and early Georgian forms, less feminine than the French and therefore perhaps nearer to Spanish work, were adopted. These were followed by the designs of Thomas Chippendale based on French rococo patterns but often combined with Chinese or Gothic elements. That English furniture was shipped to Spain and Portugal is shown in records of exportation preserved in the Public Records Office, London (91). The Portuguese trade somewhat exceeded the Spanish, possibly because of a colony of English people at O Porto engaged in the port-wine trade, or because of the more friendly relations between the two countries. Chairs, looking-glasses, clocks, joinery, and upholstered ware are listed in the records of exportation. Under joinery came tables, and under upholstery, beds, curtains, carpets, and easy chairs. Some English furniture destined for Spain differed from that for the home market. Chairs nearly always had cane seats, an unusual feature for eighteenth-century furniture, doubtless due to the Spanish climate. Many pieces were decorated with scarlet Japan lac. Chairs when lacquered, on account of cost, were usually of beech, an unsound timber requiring stretchers to strengthen the cabriole legs.

In Spain, even when using sound wood, chair makers often added stretchers, either from long habit or because they doubted the strength of the fragile-looking cabriole. Among extant pieces of Queen-Anne lacquered furniture sent to Spain, Symonds has described sets of chairs and settees, a day bed, Oriental cabinets on stands, and pier glasses which probably, in agreement with fashion, were made *en suite* with matching tables and pairs of stands. Although the demand for Oriental lacquer was strong in England, mahogany furniture, whether plain or with the raised parts gilded, was more popular. Mahogany was the wood used almost exclusively for Chippendale pieces.

An adaptation of an English eighteenth-century design by a Spanish workman is a lacquered chair (Fig. 91) at the Archæological Museum, Madrid. Although Queen-Anne style in shape, the chair shows its Spanish origin by its unusually tall back with straight, instead of curved, uprights. The central splat is flat in comparison with those of English make. As in Queen-Anne chairs, the seat is slipped into a frame to which the cabriole legs are hipped. The legs, with hoof feet and Louis-the-Fourteenth stretchers, appear more French than English in inspiration as does the rococo ornament on the back cresting. Early eighteenth-century English chair makers relied less upon carved decoration than on grace of general form. Both English and French ideas here combined with Spanish workmanship to produce a rich but hybrid effect. Another

FIGURE 92

CATALAN CHAIR
XVIII century chair with
cane seat and back.
Formerly in the collection
of Charles Deering,
Marycel, Sitges

92

hybrid chair, more emphatically Spanish in feeling, is shown in Fig. 92. Many pieces of foreign furniture, and even the style-books of famous French and English designers must have found their way to Spain.

In the *Museo Salzillo* at Murcia is a wood carving of *The Last Supper* (Fig. 93) by Francisco Salzillo y Alcáraz, to be carried in processions. The sculptor has seated his figures upon stools of Queen-Anne design but, with a Spaniard's pleasure in baroque ornament, has added deep pendant seat aprons edged with broken C-scrolls. A stool in the French taste is shown in Fig. 94.

In the second half of the eighteenth century a classical reaction gradually appeared in design. This Italian neo-classic style reached Spain by way of France. It is now called Louis the Sixteenth after the French king. In England it was first interpreted by Robert Adam, followed by Hepplewhite, Sheraton, and others. Charles the Third, who came to the Spanish throne from Naples in 1759, brought knowledge of the classic revival with him. During his reign progress in all lines of craftsmanship reached its height in Spain, only to lapse again after his death. The King's deep interest in the minor arts caused him to found royal workshops at Madrid in which excellent Louis-the-Sixteenth furnishings for palaces were turned out (92). In Spain, public notice was not focused on the work of individuals to the extent that it was in France and England. The craftsmen of the King of Spain were adapters rather than creators. Their names are recorded but have not lived as have those of the great foreign designers and cabinetmakers (93).

Late eighteenth-century pieces of furniture were even more delicate in appearance than rococo examples. The straight line replaced the curve everywhere, square tapering legs supplanting cabrioles. In ornament, natural flowers were greatly fancied. Shepherds' hats and crooks, garden tools, musical instruments, sheaves of wheat, doves and ribbons intermingled with such classical motives as quivers, husks, laurel wreaths, and battle trophies. Designs were executed with such great exactitude that they often produced a stiff and artificial effect. Gilt, lacquer, porcelain plaques, ormolu mounts, and marquetry continued to be used. Painted medallions and Wedgwood plaques were popular late in the century, especially when combined with pale satinwood veneer. Mrs. P. J. Walker of West Hartford, Connecticut, owns a fine piece of furniture of this type. It is a satinwood grand pianoforte (Fig. 95) designed by Thomas Sheraton for Manuel de Godoy to be presented to María Luisa, Queen of Spain, and manufactured by John Broadwood

FIGURE 93

CHAIR AND STOOLS

XVIII century stools shown in a carving of *The Last Supper* by Francisco Salzillo y Alcáraz in the Museo Salzillo, Murcia

and Sons of London in 1796. The pianoforte is inset with blue Wedgwood plaques, banded with mahogany, and on top is inlaid the Spanish crown in various woods. One side displays an ormolu panel embossed with the arms of Spain. This fine object must have been greatly admired in Spain, and its style was doubtless copied.

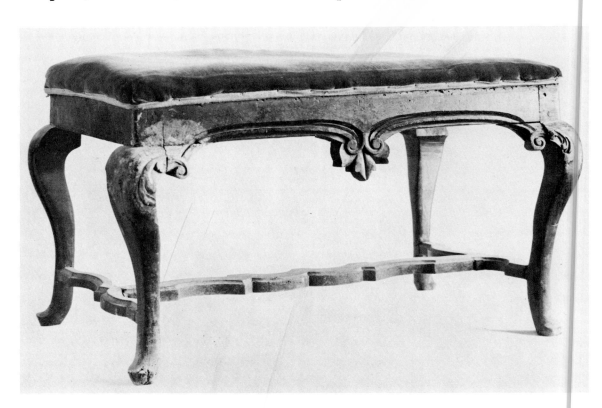

FIGURE 94

TABORET

XVIII century painted stool, showing French influence. In the Museo Episcopal, Vich

One new kind of furniture which was developed in France and adopted in Spain during Louis the Sixteenth's reign was the *vitrine*. This was a glass-enclosed wall or table cabinet to display miniature objects, usually *chinoiserie*, with which ladies of the court delighted to surround themselves. The *vitrine* exhibited these objects, which formerly were displayed on chimney pieces and tables and kept them safe from dust and breakage. A Spanish cabinet on which still persisted rococo designs, long-lived in Spain, is exhibited at The Isabella Stewart Gardner Museum (Fig. 96). French *vitrines* were less ornate, the decoration of their frames being made subordinate to that of the objects inside.

An interior furnished with Spanish pieces of Louis-the-Sixteenth inspiration is a bedroom (Fig. 97) at the *Casa Cabanyes*, Argentona. The bed is white and gold, its headboard, with the monogram of the Virgin, being hung to the wall. Bed, mirror, and set of chairs are gay and graceful in comparison with the rich and ponderous pieces of earlier times. In Spain, beds were customarily placed in the corner of the room, as shown here, or in alcoves hung with curtains (94).

French rooms during Louis the Fifteenth's reign were made smaller and more intimate than formerly with wall and ceiling decoration in harmony with the furnishings, but in Spain they continued to have the

FIGURE 95

SHERATON PIANOFORTE

Satinwood grande pianoforte made in London in 1796 as a gift for María Luisa, Queen of Spain. In the collection of Mrs. P. J. Walker, West Hartford, Connecticut

FIGURE 96

CABINET
XVIII century *vitrine* at
the Isabella Stewart
Gardner Museum, Boston

96

approximate dimensions of ballrooms until late in the century.

Major William Dalrymple, traveling in Spain in 1774, reported that while members of the nobility at Córdoba had good houses, in which there were handsome suites of apartments, the furnishings were by no means adequate, consisting of elegant mirrors, rich silk hangings, and rush-bottom chairs in the principal rooms. These houses were constructed of stone, built around courts, their owners living in the lower rooms in summer and the upper ones in winter (95).

Townsend, who visited Spain in 1786, wrote that the most magnificent house at Madrid was the Duke of Alba's, having four hundred bedrooms, but not one room suitably furnished to the rank and fortune of its lord (96). A less spacious house at Avilés described by the same author, built around a court with servants' quarters and a chapel on the ground floor, had a dining room and a drawing room, both spacious and lofty and four principal bed chambers. Of the chambers, two only were single bedded, the rest having three or sometimes four beds (97). The great hall where the family dined was fifty by twenty feet and would have been elegant if well appointed. It contained a long oak table surrounded by strong oak benches.

Another room described by Townsend was that of Antonio Ulloa at Cádiz, which was twenty by fourteen feet and about eight feet high. There was no scarcity of furniture in this room which was filled with chairs, tables, trunks, boxes, a bed, a press, carpenters' tools, clocks, pictures, mirrors, American antiquities, and many other things (98). Townsend was careful to describe the inns at which he stayed. They varied from the usual hovel with furniture broken or missing, to the rarer clean and comfortably furnished house (99).

Members of the middle class made the reception room their finest. Here they entertained at *tertulias* or evening parties where conversations were held, cards played, and refreshments enjoyed. The room was usually furnished with a settee flanked by two armchairs with side chairs placed geometrically against the walls. The rest of the house with its white-washed walls and rough straw-seated chairs was poor in comparison (100).

In the provinces away from the dominance of the French court, sturdy furniture continued to be turned out along traditional lines. A chair characteristically Spanish developed in the Levantine region at the end of the seventeenth century and became very popular during the eighteenth. It was usually built of inexpensive pine since the surface was customarily gilded and painted or lacquered red, green, ivory, or black. Red was favoured for Andalusian examples. The chairs had straight front legs turned like the tall back posts which were topped with pointed finials. The legs were connected by low stretchers, usually a splat with two turned stretchers in front. The seats were woven from rushes. The tall ladder backs were surmounted by an arched top splat bearing floral designs, religious symbols, or inscriptions. The splats below and one beneath the seat were harmoniously shaped but only slightly arched, having similar although less elaborate designs. The strong, masculine appearance of these chairs, their originality, and their brilliant colour gave them great appeal to Spanish taste. At the museum of *Cau Ferrat*, Sitges, there are a number of fine examples. The Marchioness of la Cenia at the villa of Son Verí, Mallorca, had a handsome pine chair (Fig. 98) covered with *gesso* and decorated in black and gold.

Many provincial chests continued to be made in the old form but with their carved or painted decoration brought up-to-date. Trunks with metal work shaped in rococo designs were much used and highly decorative. New metal-work patterning is the only change to be seen on an eighteenth-century leather-covered trunk and stand (Fig. 99) at The Art Institute of Chicago. Brass studs on this trunk are even more

FIGURE 97

BEDROOM
Interior showing XVIII
century painted furniture
at the Casa Cabanyes,
Argentona

98

FIGURE 98

CATALAN CHAIR
XVIII century pine side chair covered with gesso and decorated in black and gold formerly in the collection of the Marchioness of la Cenia, Mallorca

abundant than those on earlier pieces. Small trunks or boxes, products of the leather or metal worker's skill, come to light wherever Spanish travelers have been, many appearing in Mexico and South America. They date from the seventeenth and eighteenth centuries, and their special purpose can only be guessed. Some had straps inside which formed compartments for bottles, and others were plain like the trunk (S80, Fig. 199) at the Hispanic Society (101). The panels are embroidered with men in long-skirted coats, long waistcoats, tight-fitting knee breeches, and cocked hats which came into fashion after 1760 (102). Such chests are not only beautiful but also extremely sturdy, thus fulfilling two important requirements of Spanish handicraft.

Eighteenth-century methods of production changed little from those of earlier times. Tools, except perhaps in the royal workshops, were crude and old fashioned. During this century, especially in the provinces, turners were kept busy shaping parts for chairs, tables, beds, and spinning wheels. They used the bow lathe rather than the pole lathe of other countries. Such lathes are depicted on an eighteenth-century tile at the Hispanic Society (Fig.101). From the string of a bow lathe the thong twisted around the revolving stick, reaching the treadle. The worker held his chisel-like tools steadied on the rest against the turning wood when the treadle went down and he held them back when it returned to position (103). Bow lathes are still used in certain provinces of Spain. At Cáceres, a craftsman (Fig.100) uses one to turn out chairs from *madroña* wood. On the floor is a bundle of rushes for seats, and near by stands a small finished chair of traditional design. A primitive and even simpler lathe is described as used in Spain late in the eighteenth century by Townsend who said:

"I was no less struck to see the address and dispatch with which the soft-wood turners, at Alicant, execute their work. They sit on a low stage, above which the two poppet heads and points are raised six inches, and instead of a pole and treddle they use a bow; the left hand holds the tool, which they guide by the constant application of the right foot, whilst the left foot keeps the moveable poppet and point close up to the work. Such a position must be exceedingly uneasy, till custom and long habit have reconciled them to it" (104).

With such crude tools, it is not strange that Spanish furniture was less elegantly finished than French. Further proof of the continuation of primitive methods of carpentry are added by Townsend when he spoke of the artisans of Barcelona.

"The carpenters work in a manner peculiar to this city. They have neither pit saw, hand saw, carpenter's adze, axe, nor hatchet: to slit

FIGURE 99

TRUNK AND STAND
XVIII leather-covered
chest with brass studs at
The Art Institute of
Chicago

FIGURE 100

WOOD TURNER
AT LATHE (*left*)
XX century provincial
craftsman at Cáceres uses
a primitive bow lathe to
turn the leg of a chair

FIGURE 101

WOOD TURNER
AT LATHE (*right*)
XVIII century tile from
Cataluña depicts a primitive
lathe very similar to the
one in Figure 100. Tile is
in the collection of The
Hispanic Society of
America, New York

a plank, they fix it in a vice and use a spring saw strained by a bow, for working which they require two men. At this we need not wonder much; yet, when we see two men employed with the same tool, that is, with a tool of the same form, but finer, to make either dove-tail joints for cabinets, or tenants for doors and sashes, we must be allowed to smile. If they wish to smooth a board, they let it incline upon two wooden tressels, and hew it across the grain with a cooper's adze, not reflecting that an elastic body cannot resist the stroke" (105).

In spite of the crudeness of their tools, woodworkers were taking a new interest in furniture design, for at another point in his book Townsend spoke of the Academy for the Noble Arts at Barcelona where "not only the sculptor, the architect, and the engineer, but the coach-maker, the cabinet-maker, the weaver, nay even the taylor and the haberdasher, may derive great advantages from that accuracy of sight, and that fertility of invention, which are acquired by the practice of drawing and designing" (106).

The eighteenth century saw the decline of the guilds of Spain which had been so strong for nearly three hundred years. In 1707 they were deprived of their political power by Philip the Fifth (107). Ideas of industrial freedom reached Spain from revolutionary France, and early in the nineteenth century the guilds were suppressed. New and cheaper kinds of furniture were made in imitation of foreign styles.

SPANISH
AND PORTUGUESE
COLONIAL FURNITURE

V THE history of Spanish colonial furniture begins in the sixteenth century after skilled artisans and chosen colonists followed the *conquistadores*. Early adventurers, being men of war, had little need for household goods other than trunks and chests. Any decorative furniture which they brought with them was mainly for ceremonial use, an example being a hip-joint chair (Fig. 102) in which Cortés is seated while receiving the surrender of Cuahtemoc, pictured in a record by Indian artists. As soon as conquest made settlement possible, expeditions sailed from Spain with supplies of all kinds so that cities might be built and the civilization of the mother country be established in the New World. The Roman Catholic Church was an important colonizing and cultural influence in the Indies, sending skilled carpenters and sculptors across the sea to build and decorate splendid churches. The first colonial furniture was based on or copied from European models with scarcely a trace of native workmanship. At the centres of Spanish population, artisans became organized into groups patterned after the trade guilds of the Peninsula. On August 30th, 1568, ordinances for carpenters, sculptors, joiners, and makers of stringed instruments were issued by the city of Mexico. Among the strict regulations of the guild was one which forbade a workman to open a shop in the city without being examined in his trade. All wood had to be inspected, and furniture makers were segregated to a certain district in the city. A man who wished to be examined in the art of carving was required to make a writing desk with base, a French-type chair, an inlaid hip-joint chair, a turned field bed, and a table, the making of decorative furniture evidently being part of the carver's trade. Disobedience of any of the many ordinances was punishable by fines and imprisonment

yepolinhq̃ mexica

FIGURE 102

HIP-JOINT CHAIR
XVI century Aztec
painting depicts Cortés
accepting the surrender of
the chieftan Cuahtemoc

(108). An ordinance for carvers and sculptors of Mexico City dated
April 7th, 1589, stated that the rules concerning tests of skill did not
apply to Indians and that Spaniards might not buy objects made by
natives for resale (109).

Dwellings in the Indies ranged from timber or adobe huts to fine
houses as similar to those of Spain as possible. Urban houses at such
cities as Mexico were sparsely but comfortably furnished. Among the
principal rooms, reception room, main chamber, and dining room, the
first might have a rug on the floor, colourful hangings, walnut chairs,
and cushions. The typical bedroom contained a canopied bed with
columns turned, painted, and gilded, and a door-hanging of *guadamecil*.
Instead of a wardrobe, chests and coffers were used. There might also
be a small table with a cover and a secretary with drawers. Painted
secretaries were often made in Michoacán whence came many pieces of

103

fine furniture. Cedar or pine tables and benches were the customary furniture for dining rooms (110).

Plateresque and *mudéjar* designs, popular for sixteenth-century decorative colonial furniture, were principally inspired by Andalucía, since Sevilla and Cádiz were the cities in direct contact with the New World.

The woods most used for ecclesiastical and domestic furniture were mahogany and cedar. Mahogany, the ideal furniture wood, was unknown until the discovery of America, where its natural habitat is the West Indies, and on the continent, from southern Mexico through Central America to northern Colombia and Venezuela. It was used in the construction of public and private buildings and for galleons as well as for furniture (111). Cobo said that almost all the curious and lasting things which are produced in this land are of cedar, such as *retablos* for the temples, figures of saints, ceilings, cabinets, chests, and a thousand other things (112).

During the seventeenth century, Renaissance designs continued to be used, the plateresque style, as in Spain, followed by Herreran classicism. Toward the end of the century the complicated baroque style reached the colonies where it took deep root and flourished.

Church furniture, choir-stalls, sacristy presses, and benches, received greatest attention and set the pattern for domestic furniture. Among the finest choir-stalls (Fig. 103) were those built for the Monastery of *San Francisco*, Lima, Peru. Numbering one hundred thirty, they are in a loft at the entrance. The church was founded by Fray Francisco de la Cruz when Pizarro laid out the city in 1535. Work was started in 1546 and the building consecrated in 1673. The stalls were nearing completion in 1674 (113). Three stalls (S62: Figs. 191 to 194) were removed from the loft to allow space for an organ and were brought by the late Benjamin Chew of Philadelphia to the Hispanic Society where they are now exhibited. The carving is Renaissance in design with plateresque treatment of the seat panels, which are similar to the lower range of the choir stalls at the Lima Cathedral, about which Cobo wrote in 1625: ". . . they are making a hundred cedar stalls of great rarity and price, since although the craftsman has contracted to make them for 43,000 *pesos*, he has assured me that he has not been repaid for his work" (114).

Probably copied from the stalls at Lima, those at the Monastery of San Francisco do not achieve the same degree of excellence, but do pre-

FIGURE 103

CHOIR STALLS

Late XVII century choir
stalls in the Monastery of
San Francisco, Lima

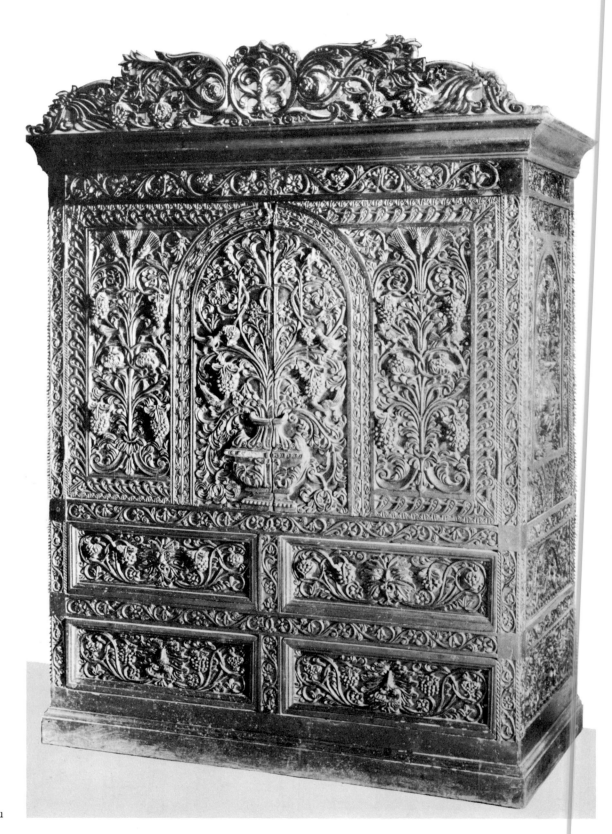

FIGURE 104

WARDROBE
XVII century carved
armario in the Palace of
the Almirante, Cuzco, Peru

106

sent the same sumptuous effect. The unevenness of skill with which the carving is executed suggests that they were the work of several artisans working under the direction of a master.

The amount of domestic furniture increased rapidly during the seventeenth century, the colonies' prosperity bringing elaborate and costly pieces of decorative furniture into the homes of the ruling classes. An *armario* in the Palace of the *Almirante de Castilla*, Cuzco, Peru, and a bench in the Church of *Santo Domingo* in the same city (Figs. 104, 105) show that although severe rectangular lines of early Spanish furniture were copied, ornament was often unrestrained. The entire surfaces are carved with floral designs suggesting the richness of Spanish plateresque carving but bolder and more confused than any work produced on the Peninsula. Heavy crestings, as shown in the illustrations, are typical of colonial workmanship. During this century *vargueños* and secretaries appeared, inlaid or veneered with choice woods, ivory, silver, tortoise shell and mother-of-pearl. The legs of tables, chairs, stands, and beds were patterned with elaborate turnings. The furnishings of a dwelling at Lima, described by Pablo Patrón are equal to any in town

FIGURE 105

CHEST BENCH
XVII century carved bench with chest base; arms missing. In the Church of Santo Domingo, Cuzco, Peru

FIGURE 106

MEXICAN CHEST
XVIII century chest at the
Art Institute of Chicago

houses of Spain, and the Palace of Chapultepec near Mexico City with its costly hangings, canopies, velvet-covered chairs, cushions, silver-laden sideboards, silver, ebony and ivory cabinets and writing desks, and elaborate beds (one described as from the Philippines) compares favourably with any Spanish royal palace (115).

The eighteenth century has given us furniture typically colonial. Native artisans working at centres where Indian culture had reached an advanced stage sometimes added traditional designs, such as the sun or snake motive of the Incas, and made slight variations in the contour of furniture lines. Decorative European birds became tropical in plumage. The eagle was sometimes replaced by the condor of the Andes. Local animals, as the puma and the llama, appeared in furniture designs; colonial flowers, fruits, and plants furnished models for Indian workmen. Aside from exaggeration of line and the introduction of American motives, native workmanship may be detected by its disregard for nicety of construction.

Spanish versions of French and English designs, the French predominating, were copied for palace furniture. The house of the Count of Regla in the street of San Felipe Neri, Mexico, contained, as did so many colonial mansions, a room of state where a portrait of Charles the Third framed in silver hung beneath a damask canopy. Below the portrait

FIGURE 107

MEXICAN CHEST
XVIII century carved chest
in the Argüeso
Collection, Madrid

stood a mahogany throne chair studded with silver and covered with crimson velvet. Around the room in formal order were placed two dozen taborets decorated with white lacquer and gilt with crimson damask seats, and at the centre of the room a mahogany table. The hangings of the apartment were silver-trimmed red damask, the large mirror frame, picture frames, ceiling beams, cornucopias, and chandelier were made of or decorated with engraved silver. The reception room of this palace had crimson velvet hangings and an *estrado* on which stood a mahogany sofa surrounded by taborets. Mirror frames, candle screens, and ceiling decorations like those in the throne room were of silver. Two mahogany consoles completed the furnishings. Although the Count of Regla's house was especially rich, walls of less pretentious houses were covered with hand-painted paper from China or imitation Cordovan leather or were painted above a dado of tiles. The room where the Countess of Regla received her intimate friends, similar to the other reception rooms in decoration, was furnished with a blue and white rug, several images of saints, a pair of two-storied, mahogany *papeleras*, a console, twenty mahogany taborets with damask seats, a harpsichord, and a painted screen with ten leaves. Next to the bedroom with its great carved and gilded bed, and its various chairs and stools, was her dressing room hung with yellow Chinese damask. The furniture consisted of a dressing

FIGURE 108

ARMCHAIR (*left*)
XVIII century chair
painted peacock blue and
gold in the Gellatly
Collection at the
Smithsonian Institution,
Washington, D.C.

FIGURE 109

CHILEAN
ARMCHAIR (*right*)
Carved armchair with
velvet covering, probably
XVIII century. In the
Convent of San Francisco,
Santiago de Chile

table with drawers and mirror with crest and frame of silver bearing her arms, a mahogany *papelera*, a spinet, and footstools of walnut upholstered with crimson damask. The candle screens, chandelier, and frame of a great mirror were silver. The least handsome room in the house was the dining room furnished with a table and stools, but the splendour of the table service made up for any lack of decorative furniture. The silverware alone required four trunks for its storage (116).

There was a strong Chinese influence in the practical arts of Mexico during the eighteenth century, not only because of the importation of goods from the East, but because a number of Chinese and Philippine artisans were employed in Mexican workshops. In the house of the Count of Regla, Chinese table porcelain, decorative urns or vases, textiles, and lacquer work testify to the popularity of Oriental goods.

At the Hispanic Society are two Mexican palace chairs of mahogany and poplar (S21, 22; Figs. 201, 202), based on French designs but unmistakably Spanish colonial in workmanship. They are probably part of a set which surrounded the throne in a room of state (117).

Furniture made for persons of moderate means was constructed along rectangular Spanish lines with the addition of rococo details in design. A Mexican chest (Fig. 106) at the Art Institute of Chicago resembles an earlier piece in construction, but the baroque scrolls on base and front are eighteenth century in pattern. Another Mexican chest (Fig. 107) in the Argüeso Collection, Madrid, is trunk shaped and unusual in that it is profusely carved with baroque scrolls resembling the embossed leather so often used to cover Mexican chests. Colonial leather workers followed Spanish methods and designs and produced many handsome hangings and furniture covers of embossed or painted leather.

Illustrating the grafting of European furniture lines on Spanish colonial objects is an armchair in the Gellatly Collection, Washington. The front legs and arm supports of the old-fashioned *sillón frailero* curve outward in sorry imitation of Louis-the-Fifteenth furniture contours (Fig. 108); another *pasticcio* appears in Fig. 109.

In Brazil, during the eighteenth century there was a strong French-Portuguese influence over furniture design. Although many fine pieces made in Brazil compare favourably with Portuguese palace furniture, a tendency toward heaviness and exaggeration of proportion may usually be seen. The extent to which this sometimes was allowed to go is illustrated by two desks and two tables (Figs. 110–113). The table in Fig. 112 is seventeenth-century Portuguese in design, but the turning of the base is more fantastic than anything produced on the Peninsula. The grotesque table in Fig. 113 is an extreme example of the distortion of Louis XV lines by native workmen. In spite of its heaviness, which was partly due to the use of American hardwoods which were difficult to work, there is an originality about eighteenth-century Spanish and Portuguese colonial furniture which was lost in later years when cabinet makers fashioned exact copies of European pieces.

Approximately the same time that Spain was exploring and colonizing the West Indies, Portugal began her colonial expansion in the East. Six years after the voyage of Columbus, Vasco da Gama rounded the Cape of Good Hope and reached the southwest coast of India. Trading posts and settlements were established along this coast during the sixteenth century to maintain a monopoly for Portugal over East Indian, Spice Island, and China trade. Commerce with the East had formerly been in the hands of Muhammadans who shipped by way of the Persian Gulf and the Red Sea, then overland to the ports of Syria and Egypt, whence the goods reached Europe in Venetian vessels. Portuguese sea control over India made Lisboa the great mart with the

FIGURE 110

BRAZILIAN
SECRETARY

In the style of João V of
Portugal (1706–50).
Formerly in the collection
of Señorita Victoria
Aguirre, Buenos Aires

East for about a hundred years. To her shores hastened Spanish, Dutch,
and English merchants to satisfy the European demand for Eastern
goods, a demand which increased until it became almost a craze during
the seventeenth century. The Portuguese failed to consolidate their
Eastern Empire and thus were unable to keep a trade monopoly after
the close of the sixteenth century. In 1597 Dutch traders invaded the
Indies, soon followed by the English who gradually stripped away
Portuguese possessions, until at the end of the seventeenth century
little was left save Goa, the capital.

Old Goa, once called "Golden", was originally a fortress in the hands of

FIGURE 111

WRITING DESK
Desk of jacaranda wood in
the style of João V of
Portugal. Formerly in the
collection of Señorita
Victoria Aguirre,
Buenos Aires

Hindus and then of Muhammadans. Alburquerque seized it for the
Portuguese in 1510. Its position under him commanded the trade of
the western coast from the Gulf of Cambay to Cape Comorin. In 1542
the city's architectural splendour was mentioned by Saint Francis
Xavier. This splendour was due to the building efforts of Franciscans,
Dominicans, Jesuits, and other missionaries who accompanied the
conquerors from Portugal. Goa received the same civil privileges as
Lisboa and attained a fabulous prosperity which reached its height
between the years 1575 and 1625. According to ancient writers, members
of the haughty ruling class placed the highest emphasis upon position

FIGURE 112

TABLE

Portuguese Colonial table,
XVII century in style,
at Bahia

and appearance, and in accordance with this, must have demanded
lavish furnishings for their dwellings (118). Guimarães and Sardoeira
stated that at such Indo-Portuguese cities as Goa and Malacar, especially during the governorship of Afonso da Alburquerque (1509-
1515), Indian and Portuguese artificers founded a great number of
shops for furniture, weaving, and other practical arts (119). The *Museu
das Janelas Verdes*, Lisboa, also designates Goa as being the centre
where furniture was made for the Portuguese people in India. An article
on this subject speaks of the many pieces of Indian provenance still
existing in Portugal, some of which display the coats of arms of Portuguese families. The close likeness of shape and technique between this
furniture and that of seventeenth-century Portugal is mentioned (120).

Old Goa is now a place of ruin and decay with palm groves replacing
its beautiful civic buildings and famous churches and convents, only a
few of which remain in any sort of repair. The abandonment of the city
was due to its unhealthy site, the government being finally transferred
in 1759 to New Goa or Panjim, five miles nearer the sea.

Before European influence made itself felt in India, practically no
furniture was used. From the first, Portuguese explorers carried examples with them, some considered worthy as gifts of friendship to
heads of states. A chair covered with brocade and studded with silver-

gilt nails was among the presents which Vasco da Gama gave to the King of Calicut during his first interview (121). Again in 1515 when Alburquerque met the King of Ormuz, he was able to fit up a reception room with a brocaded dais furnished with two chairs of crimson velvet, fringed with gold, and benches all around them covered with cushions for the captains and the governors accompanying the king (122). Such furniture brought from the West formed a basis for Hindu workers who copied the form and added their own decorative details.

That the Indians were experienced woodworkers is shown by the excellence of their wooden architecture. Duarte de Barbosa who completed a geographical treatise on the East African, Arabian, Persian and Indian coasts in 1516 noted the workmen of the great city of Cambay on the northwest coast above Goa as experts with the turning lathe producing bedsteads, chessmen, and large wooden beads (123).

FIGURE 113

TABLE

XVIII century Portuguese Colonial table at Bahia

FIGURE 114

INLAID CABINET
XVII century Indo-
Portuguese cabinet in the
Danske
Kunstindustrimuseum,
Copenhagen

Some Indian furniture is difficult to distinguish from European as it
is Western in form, purpose, and technique. It is, however, made of
native woods such as sal, teak, ebony, and a reddish wood of the rosewood type, and bears elements of Indian design. Those pieces particularly attributed to Goa are inlaid cabinets with mermaid caryatid sup-

FIGURE 115

INLAID CABINET
XVII century Indo-
Portuguese cabinet in the
Museum Meermanno
Westreenianum, The Hague

ports. Such cabinets are not to be confused with the little Italianate inlaid traveling chests which Codrington has attributed to one of the chief centres of Mughal governance in upper India, having scenic decoration comparable to the miniature paintings of Jahangir's court and probably dating from his reign (1605–1627) (124). Intricate and

117

FIGURE 116

GOAN PULPIT
XVII century carved pulpit
of the Church of Saint
Peter, Panelim, Goa

delicate but not scenic, the inlay of the Goan cabinets is more like the Moorish work with which the Portuguese had long been familiar. George Birdwood writing in 1880 spoke of inlaid furnishings in the style of the Portuguese sixteenth and seventeenth-century tarsia, which were evidently the *chefs-d'œuvre* of patient Hindu hands, as still found at Goa and nowhere else in India (125).

In form, the cabinets are similar to *vargueños*, being a chest on chest or chest on stand, but in true Eastern fashion the mouldings and architectural features are stripped away. When a chest base is used to support the cabinet, its legs are mermaid caryatids. The open stand or table sometimes has feet shaped as scrolled birds.

The cabinets are inlaid with blackwood, studded with ivory, and are fitted with pierced gilded copper or brass hardware. The edges of the drawers and sides of the cabinets have veneered borders, the veneer fastened with an oleoresinous compound instead of glue in accordance with a caste scruple (126). The inlaid decoration is of two distinct styles. One consists of interlocking circles of fine wood forming quatrefoils in an all-over pattern, studded with ivory and ebony and illustrated by a cabinet in Copenhagen (Fig. 114). The other is a design of leafy scrolls cut like veneer with templates and set into the excavated ground, shown on a piece at the *Museum Meermanno Westreenianum*, The Hague

FIGURE 117

CABINET AND TABLE
XVII century Indo-Portuguese cabinet and stand at the Victoria and Albert Museum, London

(Fig. 115) The elaborately pierced metal work, drop pulls, and bail handles of the cabinets are Western in form, and sometimes in manufacture as well. Their design is closely akin to Spanish-derived Portuguese work. Cabinetmakers in Portugal favoured the extravagant use of nail heads in decorating their native handiwork. This characteristic has been copied on a number of Goan cabinets such as the one in Fig. 115, and on cabinet S53 (Fig. 195) at the Hispanic Society, where the nail heads are simulated by dots of inlaid ivory. Cabinet S53 also has geometric inlaid borders, perhaps copied from Portuguese Hispano-Moresque design. Mermaids similar to those upholding Indo-Portuguese cabinets may still be seen carved on the seventeenth-century pulpit (Fig. 116) of the Church of Saint Peter, Panelim, Goa. Among the Goan-type cabinets in America are two at the Virginia Museum of Fine Arts, Richmond.

A handsome cabinet at the Victoria and Albert Museum, London, is known to have come from Lisboa where there is a similar cabinet at the *Academia Real de Bellas Artes* (127), a cabinet and table at the *Museu das Janelas Verdes* (128), and other examples in private collections. The Victoria and Albert Museum possesses two more Goan cabinets on stands (Fig. 117) and a table with inlaid top and drawers. A Goan table with mermaid supports appears in the foreground of Fig. 45.

These finely constructed and highly decorative cabinets and tables of redwood and golden teak with black and ivory accents which lent an exotic touch to the seventeenth-century interiors fortunate enough to contain them are still prized for their beauty and craftsmanship.

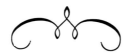

THE
HISPANIC SOCIETY
COLLECTION

COFFRET

S78

THE rectangular coffret has a hinged, pentagonal lid with sloping sides. A simple moulding borders the edges of the box. Runners, carved at the front with the fore quarters of lions regardant and at the rear with the haunches of these animals, serve as supports. The carvings which decorate the surface are executed in high relief. Around the flat top of the cover runs the following inscription: ASPICIENTES NOS

VI

FIGURE 118 (S78)

COFFRET

XV century. Walnut; height 15.7 cm (6 inches), width 31 cm (12¼ inches), depth 17 cm (6¾ inches)

121

DETAIL

Top view of the lid of the coffret, showing the carved inscription

FIGURE 119 (S58)

CHEST

Late XV century. Velvet-covered pine with iron mounts. Height, 60 cm (23½ inches), width 125.5 cm (49½ inches), depth 53 cm (21 inches)

DIMITITE QVIA SVMVS EVSTACHI IMOZ. Within the space framed by the inscription the sun, moon, and wind are carved. The full, round face at the centre is flanked by two rosettes to which the staples of the metal handle are fastened. An escutcheon, its first and fourth quarters bearing the crosses of either Alcántara or Calatrava, is centred on the front of the lid. At each side of the escutcheon appear scrolled and flowering garlands supported by boys. In one corner behind a garland crouches a hunting dog and in the other a wild beast. The sloping ends of the lid are decorated with griffins which bend down over grotesque birds resembling cranes. On the sloping back of the lid are depicted three large monsters, two winged, which are struggling with each other. At the front of the box is a lion with head deeply undercut. The keyhole of the lock pierces this figure at the base. Across the face of the box undulates a serpentine vine enlaced with curled leaves among which may be seen a number of small animal and bird grotesques. The designs on the sides of the box are of fabulous beasts and birds interrupted by leaves and acorns or cones. Across the back crouch three fantastic monsters, two of which have wings.

CHEST

S58

Crimson velvet mounted with iron covers the rectangular body and convex lid of the wooden chest. Body and lid are strapped with bars of iron which terminate in scallop shells. The lid is banded with double tracery of ogival design with *fleur-de-lis* cresting and cusped edge. Along the banding, flanking the hasps and at the corners, turreted pinnacles are placed. The arched ends of the lid and the sides of the chest are also banded with Gothic tracery. A central padlock decorated with turreted pinnacles, triangles stamped with dots, zigzags, and an incised mask, appears between two square, single-hasped shell locks with similar pinnacles and geometric patterns. Carrying handles at each end of the chest show a line, dot, and circle design of Moorish origin. The rose-coloured, flowered, silk-damask lining of the interior is not original but appears to be eighteenth century in date. Numerous private collections in Spain contain chests of this type formerly used as bridal chests or as trunks for clothing.

FIGURE 120 (S15)

ARMCHAIR
XVI–XVII century.
Walnut, with embroidered
leather back and seat (one
of three similar chairs
in the Society's collection).
Height of seat 52 cm (20½
inches), width of seat 61
cm (24 inches), depth of
seat 42.3 cm (16½ inches);
total height 100 cm (40
inches)

ARMCHAIR

S15

The leather back and seat of the *sillón frailero*, embroidered in yellow and green silk, are attached to the framework by nails with large, brass, rosette-shaped heads. At the centre of the back is an heraldic poplar leaf surrounded by a design resembling a foliated cross. At the corners, within a border of stitched lines, *fleurs-de-lis* are embroidered. The seat is upholstered over boards fastened to the side seat rails. Stitched lines divide the leather covering into four triangular sections joined at the centre by a circle decorated with a dark green velvet poplar leaf backed by a stitched and embroidered leaf-shaped figure. At the front the leather turns down in the form of an apron, embroidered with linked rosettes and a central poplar leaf.

FIGURE 121 (S55)

MUDÉJAR CHEST
(*open*)
XVI century. Walnut,
inlaid with ivory. Height
30.5 cm (12 inches).
Width 67 cm (26¼ inches),
depth 44 cm (17¼ inches)

FIGURE 122 (S55)

MUDÉJAR CHEST
(*closed*)

MUDEJAR CHEST

S55

A flared plinth supports the rectangular body of the chest. The over-hanging edge of the flat top is moulded at the front (a restoration). The central lock is without a lock plate. Bands of ivory diagonals which represent roping edge the body and lid. The bandings have been largely restored by painted instead of inlaid diagonals. Inside the chest near the top a tier of lidded boxes and shallow drawers is constructed. The boxes at the sides, above single drawers, run the entire width of the interior. Between them, across the back, is a box with two drawers in its underframing. Mosaics of geometric ivory inlay cover the surface of the chest. Front and sides are decorated alike with a central, rectangular diaper of hexagonals formed of stars and flowers. This rectangular field is surrounded by borders of zigzags, rosettes, stars, and quatrefoils. Lines of quatrefoils divide the back into three squares, each of which contains a large figure resembling a snow-flake crystal made up of minute pieces of ivory. The outer and inner surfaces of the top are patterned with circular medallions, diamonds, and hexagons, formed of stars, flowers, and quatrefoils. The plinth, the sides of the lid and the top rim of the body are inlaid with small geometric designs. The hinges and catchplate on the inner side of the lid have been painted with con-tinuations of the inlaid designs. Around the interior of the chest, above the boxes, runs a double border of geometric inlay. The boxes, including the inner surfaces of their lids, and the underframing, are also inlaid. The drawers, which have small, ivory knob pulls, are not ornamented with inlay but are painted with stars and quatrefoils. A sixteenth-century *mudéjar* chest in the collection of the Marchioness of Berme-jilla del Rey, Madrid, closely resembles this piece in construction and decoration.

FIGURE 123 (S51)

HISPANO-MORESQUE
CABINET

XVI century. Walnut with
boxwood and ivory inlay.
Height 148 cm (58¼
inches), width 102.5 cm
(40½ inches), depth 40.5
cm (15¾ inches)

HISPANO-MORESQUE CABINET

S51

The main body of the cabinet opens at the front with two doors. The outer and inner surfaces of these doors and the sides of the cabinet are inlaid with bone stars and flowers framed by Moorish interlacery of boxwood. Mouldings on the doors and sides border the inlay and form panels. A moulded cornice supports the upper story of the *armario*. This story has an undecorated top with moulded edge and inlay at the front and sides in boxwood interlacery set with bone stars in Moslem design. The hinged front swings upward to disclose a compartment with a semi-engaged column at each side of the opening. Supported by two birds with leaf-scrolled terminations, a cartouche, bearing the monogram of Christ (IHS) surrounded by flames, is inlaid in boxwood on the inner surface of the lid. The interior of the main body of the *armario* is divided into two parts. At the top are two galleries of columns, the upper with a balustrade. Between these galleries is an entablature studded with brass-headed nails cut in the shape of rosettes and four small drawers decorated with an inlaid diaper of circles made up of triangles of bone within borders of boxwood. Below the moulded cornice of the entablature runs a narrow strip of boxwood and bone inlay. Nulling and leaf moulding ornament the base of the entablature. At the centre of the lower gallery stand two columns flanking a three-centred arch supported by fluted pilasters. The soffit of the arch is cut with leaf moulding, and the spandrels are carved with cherubs' heads. Below the open galleries are drawers with moulded borders, a long one at the top, with four below at the right, and two paneled to look like four at the left. Inlay similar to that of the drawers beneath the balustrade covers the long drawer and those at the right. The drawers at the left are without inlay and have locks. Instead of the brass knobs which are fastened to the other drawers of the cabinet, these have ring pulls, one of which is missing. The back of the *armario*

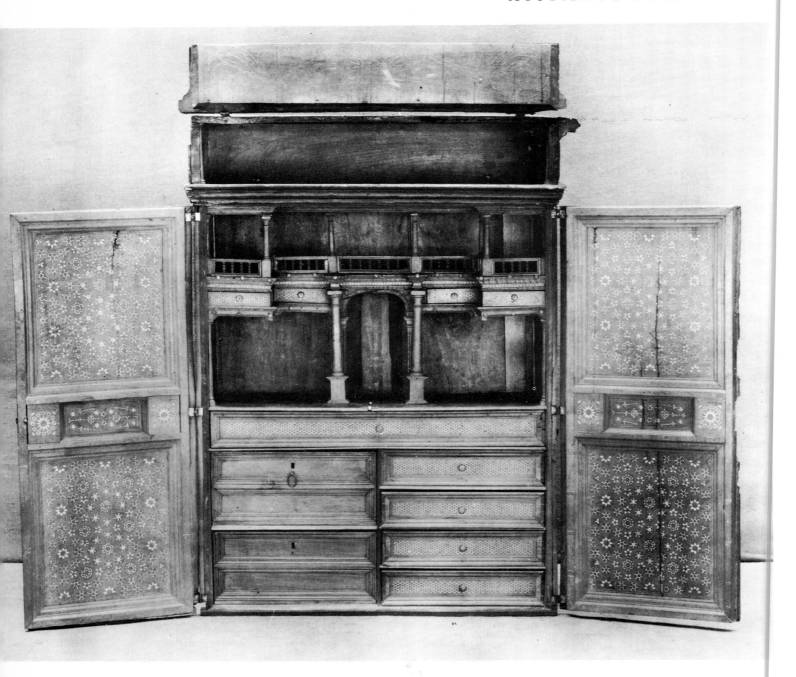

FIGURE 124 (S51)

HISPANO-MORESQUE
CABINET (*interior*)

is undecorated, for the cabinet was designed to stand against the wall.
Articles of this type were usually set upon low stands or feet. This
cabinet, because of the monogram which it bears, was probably built
for the sacristy of a church or cathedral.

130

VARGUEÑO

S47

The exterior of the cabinet is without decoration except for the single-hasped iron lock, which appears to be a seventeenth-century replacement, and a simple cornice moulding which borders the front and sides of the hinged and overhanging top. The elaborate boxwood carvings of the interior indicate that the *vargueño* is of Catalan origin. The under-side of the hinged top is divided into two squares separated by a vertical panel which has a raised and moulded walnut centre surrounded by boxwood strapwork of plain and foliated, linked S-scrolls backed by crimson satin. The middle of each square displays a pierced boxwood medallion with wreathed edge and flowered, trefoil corners showing the helmeted head of a warrior in profile silhouetted against satin. The squares are further decorated by two outer borders of pierced, foliated, boxwood strapwork, also over red satin, and by raised walnut mouldings set with boxwood beads and reels. Below the lid is a shallow compartment with a gallery at the sides and back, containing six small drawers. These drawers are separated by semi-attached, turned colonettes. They are faced with pierced, boxwood chimeric creatures flanking central urns, against satin, and are bordered by walnut mouldings. From each carved central urn is suspended a brass pull in the shape of a double-handled vase. Below the upper compartment, the interior of the

FIGURE 125 (S47)

VARGUEÑO

XVI century. Walnut with boxwood. Total height 129 cm (50¾ inches), width 110.3 cm (43½ inches), depth 47.5 cm (18¾ inches)

cabinet is fitted with ten drawers and two compartments with doors. The doors display helmeted heads of warriors in relief backed by satin. The drawers are decorated like those of the upper compartment but are larger, and their chimeric figures with scrolled plumage are carved with greater elaboration. Upon the inner side of the drop lid is inlaid an Arabic geometric pattern in boxwood. An arcaded trestle stand with fluted columns and colonettes supports the cabinet.

FIGURE 126 (S47)

VARGUEÑO (*interior*)

133

FIGURE 127 (S42)

VARGUEÑO

XVI century. Walnut with boxwood and ivory inlay. Total height 138 cm (54½ inches), width 96 cm (38 inches), depth 44.5 cm (17½ inches)

134

VARGUEÑO

S42

Inlay of ivory and minute strips of light wood, probably box, decorates the *vargueño* cabinet. Upon the outside of the drop lid is represented the façade of a brick building. This has a large central portal with triangular, ivory-studded pediment above an arched door covered with ivory nail heads. The portal is flanked by two grilled windows beneath shell-hooded crestings. The façade appears to project beyond the windows in wings faced with small inlaid doors of classic design. Above these doors is inlaid a row of spindles supported upon colonettes which are interrupted by stars and foliated scrolls. The spindles are topped by bricked arches with pointed central crestings and turrets between which stand tall, slim crosses. In the middle of the drop lid a coat of arms has been applied. Its second and third quarterings are obliterated. The first shows a *lion rampant within a bordure charged with eight roundels*, and the fourth quarter, *three cauldrons within a bordure charged with seven roundels*. On each side of the escutcheon appear flowers, roundels, stars, scrolls, and a vase of stiff, daisy-like flowers within a shell-hooded niche. Above the coat of arms runs an arcade, framing stars and rosettes. An inlaid cable border and an applied beveled moulding, set with chevrons, surround the drop lid. On the inner side of the drop lid is inlaid a wheel-like figure centred by a star from which radiate columnar spokes separated by vase-shaped foliated scrolls resembling budding vines. Around the outside of the central wheel curl a profusion of similar scrolls, some with budded ends and others terminating in horns. The top of the cabinet is hinged and may be lifted back against the wall. Its outer decoration corresponds to that on the interior of the drop lid. On the inside of the hinged top is a row of colonettes, the spaces between containing alternately an urn with flowers and a rosette with scrolls at top and base. These colonettes support an upper row of smaller columns upholding an arcade, each arch of which frames a conventional foliation or a vase with stiff flowers. The sides of the cabinet are fitted with drop handles and are inlaid with

FIGURE 128 (S42)

VARGUEÑO (*interior*)

a circle filled by an interlaced, geometric, star pattern. The hinged lid is affixed to the sides of the cabinet by hooks, while the drop front is fastened by modern inner button catches. When the top is lifted, a box-like compartment appears, faced with a panel inlaid with ivory rosettes, which is framed by an applied moulding inlaid with chevrons. The cabinet contains ten drawers with brass, vase-shaped, drop pulls and two compartments with doors. On each door is a brick wall with a portal, similar to the central one on the drop lid, surrounded by an inlaid cable border. Two of the drawers are inlaid with round arches.

136

Another displays an arcade supported by colonettes framing urns and flowers. On the remaining drawers rosettes, stars, urns, and budded scrolls are inlaid. The trestle stand of the cabinet has vase-turned and fluted columnar legs and two twisted central pillars to which the arcaded cross brace is fastened.

COAT OF ARMS
Enlarged view of inlaid coat of arms on front of *vargueño* S42 (Fig. 127)

137

FIGURE 129 (S74)

VARGUEÑO

Early XVII century.
Walnut, with gilded iron
mounts backed by modern
red velvet. Total height
137.7 cm (54¼ inches),
width 110.8 cm (43¾
inches), depth 41.5 cm
(16½ inches)

VARGUEÑO

S74

(*See also Frontispiece*)

The design of the pierced iron mounts on the exterior of the cabinet is based upon scrolls and *fleurs-de-lis* resembling patterns used by ironsmiths of the School of Madrid. The balustered plate of the single-hasped lock is shield-shaped pierced with scrolls and *fleurs-de-lis* at crest and base. As usual, the mountings are fitted with baluster drop pulls, cone-shaped bosses, and push bolts. The interior of the cabinet is brilliantly gilded. The moulded partitions and mouldings around the eleven drawer fronts and two compartment doors, as well as the majority of the decorative carvings, glitter with gold. In the centre is a shallow opening to accommodate inkwells and writing materials, which has a three-centred arch with red and black ground and gilt moulding, upheld by gold and blue, fluted pilasters. The faces of the drawers and doors are likewise painted red streaked with black, and each contains an iron knob pull. On the drawers in the two upper rows, gilded central cartouches are carved. The cartouches of the top row are supported by polychromed boys holding gilded cornucopias filled with gold and brown fruit. On the long centre drawer of the tier below, the central cartouche is flanked by two reclining female figures dressed in pink cloaks and green robes barred with gold *estofado*. Each holds a ribbon from which is suspended a cluster of fruit. The drawers on each side display cartouches with swags of drapery and fruit. Two narrow drawers above the open central compartment are centred with gilded rams' heads, their curved horns upholding fruit in draperies. Each of the three bottom drawers bears a gilded lion's head grasping in its teeth the stems of scrolled, gold and brown, conventionalized flowers. The compartment doors, which have small keyholes, are decorated by large green and gold carved cartouches containing coats of arms. The arms at the left, *azure, a tower proper supported by two lions rampant or, with five fleurs-de-lis azure,* appear to be those of the Mogrovejo family, described by Piferrer as *sable, a tower argent with windows azure, surmounted by three fleurs-de-lis or, and supported by two lions rampant, the bordure gules charged with eight T's.* The arms at the right may be those of the Robres family: *azure, an oak tree eradicated proper supported by two dogs rampant*

139

FIGURE 130 (S74)

COAT OF ARMS (*left*)
Carved on the door of the *vargueño* in Figure 129, the arms appear to be those of the Mogrovejo family

FIGURE 131 (S74)

COAT OF ARMS (*right*)
Carved on the door of the *vargueño* in Figure 129, the arms may be those of the Robres family

sable, langued and tied to the tree with a rope gules, a dexter arm wrapped of the last holding a key upward or. According to Piferrer, the Robres and Mogrovejo families were joined by the marriage of Doña María de Robres to Don Francisco de Mogrovejo. The stiles and rails and mullions of the cupboard stand display raised ovals simulating inlay, painted white with blue borders and red floriations. These are surrounded and connected by gilded strapwork. The corners and intersections of the stiles, rails, and mullions are reënforced with gilded mounts, pierced with volutes and *fleurs-de-lis* and attached by gilded bosses, above painted crimson grounds. In the top rail are pulls ending in the gilded heads of grotesque beasts. The stand has a moulded and gilded top edge and contains two upper drawers and a lower compartment with two doors. The interior was formerly painted red, traces of which remain. Raised and gilded mouldings divide the doors and drawers into the customary lozenge motive. The ends of the stand are paneled and are fitted with gilded-iron carrying handles with mounts backed by red paint instead of velvet. The base rails at the sides are valanced and the square feet are fluted at the front.

VARGUEÑO

S43

The cabinet is upheld by an arcaded trestle stand with grotesque animal-head pulls. This stand has slender, turned legs and heavy, central columns with spiral reedings, to which the cross brace is attached. Between the plain bottom rail and the paneled, arcaded top rail of the cross brace stand turned colonettes. Mounts of pierced iron against modern red velvet are attached to the exterior of the cabinet. In the middle of the drop lid is a large iron lock with a long, double hasp. Both lock box and hasp are decorated with spirally twisted pinnacles, those of the hasp terminating in cockleshells radiating downward. The hexagonal lock plate, perforated with delicate scrolls, displays two lions rampant. It is backed by red velvet which is edged with iron roping fastened by many small nails with pointed heads. The lock plate is surrounded by five, pierced, diamond-shaped, iron mounts over velvet the upper two centred by baluster drop pulls and the lower three by cone-shaped bosses. Four push bolts at the sides are placed above velvet-backed, pentagonal mounts pierced with scrolls and lions regardant. The narrow angle braces, hook plates, and edge mountings are of perforated, scrolled ironwork with velvet backing and *fleur-de-lis* ends. At the base of the drop lid two groups of three nails with cockleshell heads are driven through from the front to fasten the inner hinges. Carrying handles at the sides are set above scrolled octagonal mounts backed by red velvet. The interior is fitted with fourteen large drawers, four small square inner drawers, and six shallow, secret drawers. It also contains five compartments with doors, one in each corner and one in the middle. The partitions separating the drawers and doors are moulded and carved with reeded diagonals which are gilded and outlined in blue. Around each compartment door runs a border of gilded diagonals and rectangular, bone plaques painted with black facets. The doors are designed as porticoes with a pair of twisted colonettes at each side. Scrolled, fluted and gilded brackets support the colonettes, which, in turn, uphold a cornice inlaid with oval plaques of bone faceted in black.

141

FIGURE 132 (S43)

VARGUEÑO

XVII century. Walnut, with gilded iron mounts backed by modern red velvet. Total height 155 cm (61 inches), width 111.5 cm (44 inches), depth 40 cm (15¾ inches)

142

FIGURE 133 (S43)

VARGUEÑO (*interior*)

A broken and scrolled, gilded pediment and end finials of turned bone surmount the cornice. All the mouldings on the doors and drawers are gilded. The door of the large central compartment bears three colonettes at each side instead of two. Behind this door are four drawers decorated with gilded diagonals, mouldings, and faceted bone inlay. Unlike the gilded shell pulls on the other drawers, these are gilded iron knobs. The ornamentation of the four drawers surrounding the central compartment is similar to that of the doors. They lack outer borders and brackets and have triangular and raised oval bone plaques which are faceted and connected by gilded mouldings. Inlaid and gilded squares of wood are applied to the ends of the secret drawers in the lower sections. The projections are used as pulls. Between the raised squares is an inlaid panel. On the remaining drawers of the cabinet appear raised, oval, bone plaques faceted in black and joined by gilded strapwork. These drawers have pairs of bone colonettes at each end which rest upon moulded bases and uphold moulded cornices inlaid with oval and triangular faceted plaques of bone.

143

FIGURE 134 (S45)

VARGUEÑO
XVII century. Walnut
with iron mounts backed
by red velvet. Total height
146.5 cm (57¾ inches),
width 105.5 cm (41.6
inches), depth 43.5 cm
(17 inches)

144

VARGUEÑO

S45

The exterior of the cabinet bears the usual pierced iron mountings, double-hasped lock, handles, bolts, hooks, and decorative nail heads. In addition, the front displays three bosses in the shape of masks. Two of these flank the lock and the third centres the mount below. Inside are twelve drawers, four secret drawers, and two compartments with doors, separated by moulded partitions. The cupboard doors and the drawers with secret compartments are faced with small, turned colonettes of bone painted with black flutings. Two of these drawers resemble portals, having broken and scrolled pediments and turned bone finials. At the centre of each portal stands a black-lined bone cross inlaid beneath a gilded shell hood. Geometric bone inlay, faceted with black and, at intervals, raised by gilt borders, forms the principal decoration of the remaining drawers. The mouldings around the doors and seven of the drawers are unpainted, but the entablature mouldings, pediments, brackets, borders, and raised diagonals are gilded, as are the oval iron keyhole escutcheons of the doors and the cockleshell drawer pulls. An arcaded trestle stand supports the cabinet.

FIGURE 135 (S45)

VARGUEÑO (*interior*)

FIGURE 136 (S46)

VARGUEÑO

XVII century. Walnut,
with iron mounts backed
by red velvet. Total height
140 cm (55¼ inches),
width 104 cm (41 inches),
depth 41.5 cm (16½
inches)

VARGUEÑO

S46

The pierced, heraldic plate of the long, double-hasped lock and the conventional mountings on the exterior of the cabinet are backed by worn and faded red velvet edged with gilded, zigzag braid. The interior, in better condition than the outside, glitters with gold which coats the mouldings, entablature, broken and scrolled pediments of two drawers and doors, the brackets, the corrugations, and the flutings of the twisted bone colonettes, some of which are topped by knob finials. There are thirteen large drawers, three small secret drawers, and two compartments with doors. The geometric inlay which adorns them consists of raised ovals of bone faceted in black and connected by gilded strapwork, as well as flat bone plaques in the form of lozenges, rectangles, ovals, and triangles, also faceted. Strips of iron reënforce the lower corners of the chest base above runners which form feet. In the top rail below an overhanging edge are two square pulls fitted with small, brass ring handles. Simulated bone inlay faceted with black and joined by raised, gilded strapwork decorates the stiles, rails, and mullions. The stand is divided into two upper drawers and a bottom compartment with two doors.

FIGURE 137 (S46)

VARGUEÑO (*interior*)

147

FIGURE 138 (S76)

VARGUEÑO

XVII century. Walnut, with gilded iron mounts backed by modern red velvet. Total height 151.5 cm (59¾ inches), width 110.5 cm (43½ inches), depth 41 cm (16 inches)

148

VARGUEÑO

S76

The exterior of the cabinet displays the traditional decorative iron-work, its gilded mountings delicately pierced with fine scrolls above red velvet which is not original. Inside are fifteen large drawers, six small, disguised drawers, and four compartments with doors. These are bright with gilded mouldings, imbrications, roping, brackets, and pediments and are further ornamented by geometric bone inlay and pairs of twisted bone colonettes. Most of the inlay consists of raised rectangles of bone faceted with black, surrounded by gilt borders, and joined together by gilded strapwork. Each drawer has a gilded iron cockleshell pull. The doors, one in each corner, are built like miniature porticoes, as are four drawers surrounding the centre. These drawers differ from the doors by having disguised compartments in their bases instead of brackets, a dissimilar arrangement of inlaid decoration, and gilded shell hoods carved above their central pulls. The partitions between doors and drawers are moulded and faced with inlay of bone.

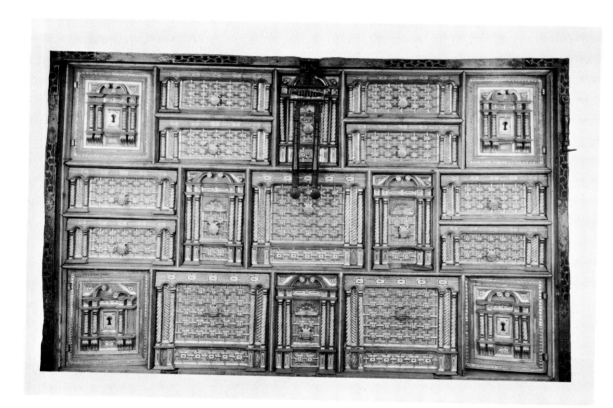

FIGURE 139 (S76)

VARGUEÑO (*interior*)

149

FIGURE 140 (S44)

VARGUEÑO

XVII century. Walnut, with gilded iron mounts backed by red velvet. Total height 144.5 cm (57½ inches), width 104 cm (41 inches), depth 42 cm (16½ inches)

VARGUEÑO

S44

The cabinet is secured by a large, double-hasped, turreted lock. Its hexagonal backplate, pierced with scrolls, *fleurs-de-lis*, and faintly indicated lions rampant, is placed against red velvet. Other ironwork appearing on the exterior consists of the customary baluster drop pulls, push bolts, hooks, cone-shaped bosses, and side handles, with their decorative, pierced mountings backed by velvet. Iron roping which originally bordered the large, geometric mounts has been replaced by braid. All the ironwork is gilded. Inside the cabinet are thirteen drawers fitted with shell pulls, three small secret drawers, and two compartments with doors. At the sides of the doors and drawers, stand pairs of twisted bone colonettes. The doors and the two drawers adjoining them are surmounted by broken and scrolled pediments placed against blue grounds on which birds and flowers are painted in white. Gilded shell hoods, above inlaid, gilt-bordered, bone quatrefoils painted with black flowers, centre the two pedimented drawers. The remaining drawers display raised, oval plaques of bone, each painted with flowers on leafy stems, or a bird touching its beak to a stem, backed by a stalk of foliage.

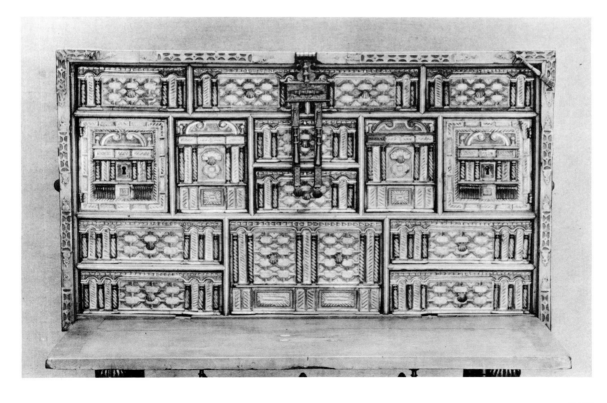

FIGURE 141 (S44)

VARGUEÑO (*interior*)

151

FIGURE 142 (S48)

VARGUEÑO

XVII century. Walnut,
with iron mounts backed
by red velvet. Total height
152.5 cm (60 inches),
width 111.7 cm (44 inches),
depth 41 cm (16 inches)

VARGUEÑO

S48

Pierced iron mounts over red velvet, a large double-hasped lock, pulls, bosses, hooks, bolts, angle braces, and side handles are fastened to the exterior of the cabinet. Inside are thirteen large drawers, seven secret drawers, and three compartments with doors, the middle one containing two drawers paneled to look like four. These central, inner drawers have simple knob pulls instead of the gilded cockleshells attached to the other drawers of the cabinet. The doors and drawers with secret compartments are surmounted by broken and scrolled pediments and resemble porticoes. All the inlaid drawer and door fronts display twisted colonettes of gilded bone, gilded mouldings, borders, corrugations, and strapwork. Facets or conventional flower designs are painted on the decorative bone inlay. The stiles, rails, and mullions at the front of the cabinet base are painted red and are inlaid with raised ovals and triangles of bone, which are faceted with black paint and bordered and connected by gilded strapwork. In the stand are two upper drawers with large iron knob pulls and a lower compartment with two doors.

FIGURE 143 (S48)

VARGUEÑO (*interior*)

153

FIGURE 144 (S75)

VARGUEÑO

XVII century. Walnut,
with gilded iron mounts
backed by red velvet. The
cupboard stand contains
an upper drawer, paneled
to look like two, and a
lower compartment with
two hinged doors. Total
height 149.5 cm (59
inches), width 105.5 cm
(41½ inches), depth
43.5 cm (17 inches)

154

VARGUEÑO

S75

The gilded iron mounts of the drop lid are backed by scarlet, modern velvet, but the handle plates at the sides of the cabinet are attached to their original, dark red velvet backing which is badly worn. Gilt braid frames the large geometric mounts. This braid probably replaces the iron roping which was customarily used for borders, as traces of earlier nail holes may be seen surrounding the mounts. The velvet ground of the double-hasped central lock and plate is missing. Within the cabinet are twelve large drawers, two of them built like porticoes with secret drawers in their bases. There is also a central compartment containing three inner drawers. The compartment door has been treated architecturally with a broken and scrolled pediment, turned finials of bone, and six twisted and gilded bone colonettes, two of which are against blue-painted backgrounds, set upon scrolled, gilded brackets. Its inlaid bone decoration, triangular or rectangular in shape, is painted with black guilloches, field flowers, rosettes, or scrolls. The drawers inside this compartment are inlaid with squares of bone painted with black, scrolled designs and edged with raised, gilded mouldings.

FIGURE 145 (S75)

VARGUEÑO (*interior*)

FIGURE 146 (S77)

VARGUEÑO

XVII century. Walnut
with gilded iron mounts
backed by modern red
velvet. Total height
157 cm (61¾ inches),
width 113 cm (44½
inches), depth 42 cm
(16½ inches)

156

VARGUEÑO

S77

The original cloth, backing the conventionalized, pierced, gilded iron mounts and heraldic lock plate, has been replaced by modern red velvet. Inside the cabinet are thirteen drawers, five of which contain secret receptacles in their bases. There are also three compartments with doors, the large central one enclosing three inner drawers paneled to simulate six. In the middle of each of the six panels facing the inner drawers is a raised rectangle of bone etched in black with the figure of an animal. Three of the panels show a dog in pursuit, and the others, from top to bottom, display a boar, a rabbit, and a panther in flight. The backgrounds of the drawers and the partitions between them are faced with bone etched with scrolled leafage. All the drawers of the cabinet are fitted with gilded iron cockleshell pulls. The partitions within the cabinet are striped with bone diagonals. Roughly carved and heavily gilded imbrications, diagonals, and beading surround the front of the large central door. Upon this door is a gilded entablature

FIGURE 147 (S77)

VARGUEÑO (*interior*)

157

and pediment upheld by two pairs of twisted bone colonettes. Bone inlay which decorates the door is etched with foliations and poorly executed, conventionalized flowers. A rectangular piece of ivory in the centre of the base of the door shows a mask from which swags of drapery are suspended. The two smaller doors are surrounded by similar gilded mouldings. They have simple entablatures supported on twisted and gilded bone colonettes with knob finials and inlaid plaques with conventionalized flowers. Each of the three doors possesses a central keyhole with a square, gilded iron escutcheon plate. The drawers on each side of the central compartment display a roundel of bone etched with a flower in the middle. A leaping fox is etched on the oval inlay which centres their secret compartments. The drawers of the top row and two in the row below are divided into square panels each bearing a raised oval of bone etched with a crested bird. Three large drawers in the bottom row are similarly treated, but display central ovals etched with classic wreathed heads in silhouette, and in their bases are gilded secret drawers on the bone plaques of which are etched leaves, dogs running in the woods, and in one case a stag. The inlay of the cupboard stand is like that of the cabinet above. At intervals along the stiles, rails, and mullions are inlaid flat bone rectangles etched with animals in woodland scenes. Each rectangle contains one figure. Dogs are pictured in pursuit of boars, rabbits, stags, foxes, and panthers. Cactus plants appear as foliage on two of the plaques. Between the inlaid plaques are strips of gilded diagonals or roping and, where the central rail and mullion cross, appear four gilded, carved rosettes.

FIGURE 148 (S77)

VARGUEÑO (*interior*)
Drawers in compartment behind door at top center of Fig. 147

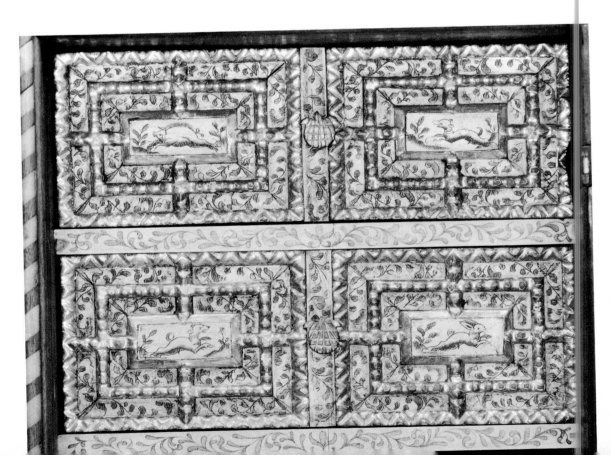

PAPELERA

S50

The *papelera*, built like a *vargueño* cabinet without the drop lid, is bound with iron and supported by pear-shaped feet. It is fitted with eight drawers, one of which is a secret compartment set in the base of the deep central drawer. The angle braces, edge mountings, and handle plates are pierced iron backed by red velvet. Nails with star-shaped heads flank the edge mounts. The drawers have oval keyhole escutcheons. At each side of the locks are cone pulls. All the ironwork was formerly gilded but only traces of the gilding now remain. The partitions separating the drawers are moulded and inlaid with strips of bone. The long, narrow drawer fronts are inlaid with raised bone plaques joined by strapwork, with bone lozenges in the intervals. At each end of the drawers, standing on moulded bases and supporting moulded cornices above, are two twisted colonettes of bone separated by diagonal reedings. A row of linked, bone rectangles runs along the drawer tops. Strapwork, mouldings, and reedings are gilded. The face of the deep central drawer resembles a portico with a pair of twisted, bone columns at each side. Originally it was topped by a broken and scrolled pediment, now missing. Its base, containing a shallow, secret drawer without pulls, is inlaid with bone lozenges and rectangles.

FIGURE 149 (S50)

PAPELERA

XVII century. Walnut and iron. *Papeleras* usually stood on tables like the one in Fig. 156. Height 44 cm (17¼ inches), width 62 cm (24½ inches), depth 33 cm (13 inches)

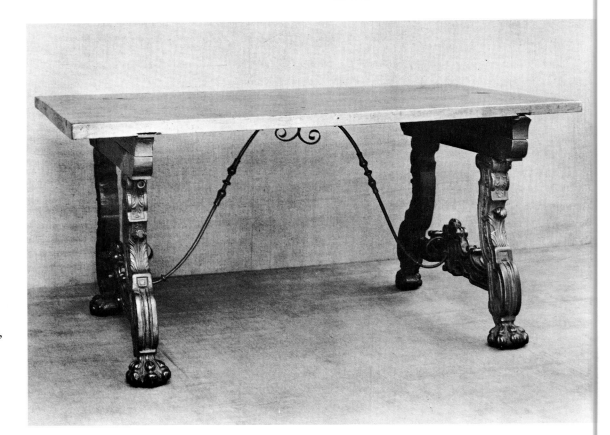

FIGURE 150 (S40)

TABLE

XVII century. Walnut, with strongly carved trestles supporting a thick, massive one-plank top. Height 86.5 cm (34 inches), width 100.5 cm (39½ inches), length 173.5 cm (68½ inches)

FIGURE 151 (S26)

TABLE

XVII century. Walnut. Height 84 cm (33 inches), width 77.5 cm (30½ inches), length 136 cm (53½ inches)

TABLE

S40

The supports upholding the top plank are constructed as trestles, somewhat lyre shaped in contour. The moulded legs are carved with acanthus sprays and pendant husks of leafage above paw feet. *Fleuron*-crested stretchers connecting the legs are centred with cartouches from which sprays of acanthus unfold. The iron baluster braces of the table have scrolled ends.

TABLE

S26

The table has a plain, rectangular top, placed upon lyre-shaped trestle legs, connected by scrolled end stretchers and braced with curved, wrought-iron baluster supports. It is possible to take the table apart by loosening turn bolts which hold the end trestles to moulded transverse pieces of wood dovetailed to the underside of the top. The ironwork is also removable. Of like style is a table at the Museum of Decorative Arts, Madrid.

FIGURE 152 (S33)

TABLE

XVII century. Walnut.
Height 80.4 cm (31¾
inches), width 94.5 cm
(37¼ inches), length
135.2 cm (53¼ inches)

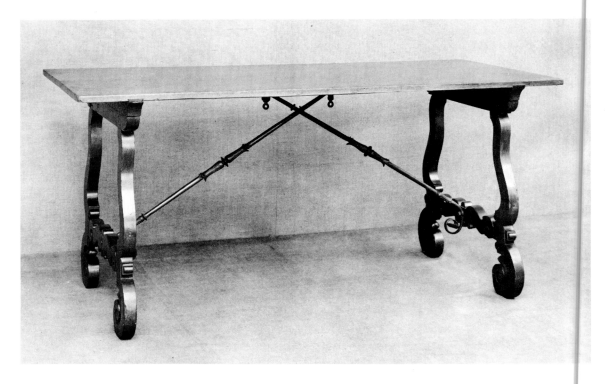

FIGURE 153 (S72)

TABLE

XVII century. An unusual
example because it is
fashioned from mahogany
instead of walnut. Height
82.5 cm (32½ inches),
width 79 cm (31 inches),
length 173 cm (68¼
inches)

TABLE

S33

Lyre-shaped trestle ends with scrolled stretchers, each bearing a central, turned and blocked spindle, uphold the undecorated top. The legs which are braced by wrought-iron balusters are carved at the front with a single acanthus leaf curled at the tip.

TABLE

S72

To the underside of the table top is attached a horizontal bar of wood to which crossed, spindle irons bracing the end trestles are screwed. These straight spindles, which are curled at the base, are decorated with leafage. The feet and stretchers of the lyre end pieces are shaped in graceful scrolls.

FIGURE 154 (S73)

TABLE

XVII century. Walnut, with lyre-shaped trestle supports. Height 76 cm (30 inches), width 80 cm (31½ inches), length 162 cm (63¾ inches)

FIGURE 155 (S39)

TABLE

XVII century. Walnut, with scrolled, lyre-shaped, flat supports; valanced iron stretchers bearing central balusters. Height 81 cm (32 inches), width 74 cm (29 inches), length 110 cm (43¼ inches)

164

TABLE

S73

The table is undecorated except for the scrolling of iron spindle braces and the shaping of lyre trestle supports. The parts may be easily separated from each other by loosening the screws.

TABLE

S39

The lower edges of the crosspieces attached to the underside of the plain top are scalloped. To these pieces are fastened scrolled, lyre-shaped, flat supports with valanced stretchers bearing central balusters. Scrolled wrought-iron spindles brace the ends.

FIGURE 156 (S27)

TABLE

XVII century. Walnut, with turned and blocked legs, connected at centre and base by valanced stretchers. Tables like this are commonly used as stands for *papeleras*. Height 76.5 cm (30¼ inches), width 42.5 cm (16½ inches), length 110 cm (43¼ inches)

FIGURE 157 (S37)

TABLE

XVII century. Walnut, with reeded and fluted columnar legs joined by valanced stretchers. Height 77 cm (30¼ inches), width 77 cm (30¼ inches), length 123.2 cm (48½ inches)

166

TABLE

S27

The narrow, undecorated top is fastened to iron-braced, removable trestle supports which have turned and blocked legs, slightly raked, and connected at centre and base by valanced stretchers. Such tables were commonly used as stands for *vargueño* cabinets, *papeleras*, or chests.

TABLE

S37

Slightly raked, reeded and fluted, columnar legs joined by valanced stretchers support the straight-edged top which has dovetailed end extensions paneled on the underside. The curved wrought-iron spindle braces, like the other parts of the table, may be removed by loosening the turn bolts. A table in the collection of The Detroit Institute of Arts is similar in construction.

FIGURE 158 (S31)

TABLE

XVII century. Walnut, the massive, single-plank top supported by reel-turned and blocked, canted legs; the curved wrought iron braces are decorated at the centre with flat, pierced, S-scrolled ornaments. Height 79.4 cm (31¼ inches), width 92.5 cm (36½ inches), length 139.5 cm (55 inches)

FIGURE 159 (S36)

TABLE

XVII century. Walnut; splayed, turned and blocked legs with turned and blocked cross stretchers and ball feet. Height 78 cm (30¾ inches), width 77 cm (30¼ inches), length 124.5 cm (49½ inches)

168

TABLE

S31

Reel-turned and blocked, canted legs arranged as trestle supports are attached to the rectangular, straight-edged top. From the turned stretcher of each end piece a curved wrought-iron brace, decorated at the centre with a flat, pierced, S-scrolled ornament, rises to the underside of the top. These braces pass each other and curve to widely separated points beneath the table top.

TABLE

S36

Beneath each end of the top are dovetailed moulded blocks to which are attached splayed, turned, and blocked legs with turned and blocked cross stretchers and ball feet. Scrolled wrought-iron balusters similar to those of S31 reënforce the end pieces.

FIGURE 160 (S24)

TABLE

XVII century. Walnut; baluster-turned and raked trestle legs on ball feet, connected by valanced end stretchers. Like S32, this table resembles one in the Salamanca Cathedral. Height 84 cm (33 inches), width 104.5 cm (41¼ inches), length 163 cm (64¼ inches)

FIGURE 161 (S32)

TABLE

XVII century. Walnut, with turned and raked legs upon pear-shaped feet connected by end stretchers, decorated on the outside with a double line of chip carving. Resembles a table in the Cathedral at Salamanca. Height 82 cm (32¼ inches), width 84 cm (31 inches), length 130.5 cm (51½ inches)

170

TABLE

S24

The baluster-turned and raked trestle legs which uphold the massive rectangular top of the table rest upon ball feet. They are connected by valanced end stretchers, housed in blocks carved with raised lozenges. Leaf tendrils ornament the scrolled baluster braces of wrought iron. A similar table may be seen at Salamanca Cathedral.

TABLE

S32

Turned and raked legs resting upon pear-shaped feet sustain the straight-edged top. Each pair of legs has a connecting end stretcher, valanced, and decorated on the outside with a double line of chip carving. The stretchers are housed in blocks which are carved on three sides with panels centred by lozenges. The scrolled baluster irons curl at the base into leaf-shaped ends. Although smaller, this table is similar to S24 and likewise resembles a table in the chapter room of the Cathedral of Salamanca.

FIGURE 162 (S30)

TABLE

XVII century. Walnut, with a heavy single plank top, resting on unusual raked trestle ends connected by S-scrolled, wrought-iron braces. Height 82.3 cm (32¼ inches), width 96 cm (37¾ inches), length 192.5 cm (6 feet, 4 inches)

FIGURE 163 (S34)

TABLE

XVII century. Walnut, fitted with three drawers decorated by rectangular panels edged with carved leaf designs. Height 84.8 cm (33½ inches), width 91.5 cm (36 inches), length 167 cm (65¾ inches)

172

TABLE

S30

The top, a single plank, rests upon raked, trestle ends connected by S-scrolled, wrought-iron braces. A deeply incised line traces the contour of the winged legs and shaped stretchers.

TABLE

S34

Beneath the plain, overhanging top is an underframing fitted with three drawers. The drawer fronts are decorated by rectangular panels edged with carved imbrications designed as leafage. In the centres of these panels are diamond-shaped iron keyhole escutcheons, likewise bordered by carved leafage. On either side of the diamonds appear raised, square rosettes centred by iron drop pulls. A border of leafage ornaments the top of the out-flaring lower edge of the underframing. The back frieze is divided into three sections corresponding to the drawer fronts. These are paneled with rectangular borders of leafage. Heavy, turned and blocked legs with bun feet, joined by low stretchers, support the table.

FIGURE 164 (S35)

TABLE

XVII century. Walnut, fitted with three drawers carved with two pairs of round rosettes edged with gouging. Height 78 cm (30¾ inches), width 81.3 cm (32 inches), length 215.2 cm (7 feet, ¾ inch)

FIGURE 165 (S25)

TABLE

XVII century. Walnut, fitted with four drawers with wooden knobs, ornamented by raised mouldings. Height 83 cm (32¾ inches), width 78.5 cm (31 inches), length 190 cm (6 feet, 3 inches)

174

TABLE

S35

Each of the three drawers in the underframing of the table is carved with two pairs of round rosettes edged with gouging. In the free central space on each drawer front appears an arch made of imbrications resembling a garland of husks. In the middle of two of the drawers are keyhole escutcheons, one being a later addition. Each drawer has two wooden knob pulls. The backs of the drawers are similarly carved but the central space on each is plain and is flanked by vertical lines of gouging. Around the bottom of the table's underframing is a flared moulding. The table rests upon turned and blocked legs joined by low stretchers.

TABLE

S25

The underframing of the table contains four drawers ornamented by raised mouldings and fitted with pairs of wooden knob pulls. Moulded brackets, dovetailed to the underside of the rectangular top, frame the drawers and the undecorated panels of the back frieze. The lower edge of the underframing is moulded. Heavy trestle supports, lyre shaped in contour, uphold the body of the table. They are strengthened by spirally twisted wrought-iron braces.

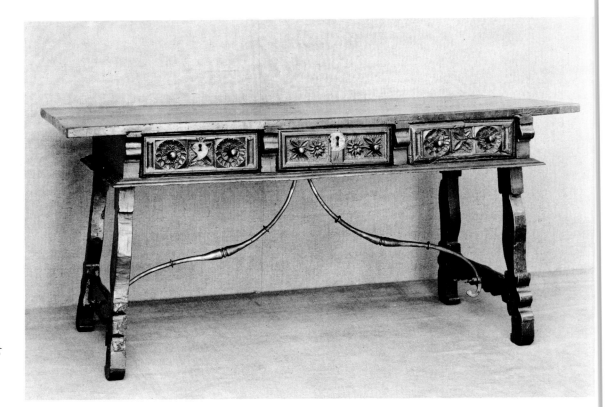

FIGURE 166 (S28)

TABLE (*front view*)
XVII century. Walnut,
with slightly canted legs,
fitted with three drawers
separated by moulded
blocks. Height 82 cm (32¼
inches), width 76.5 cm
(30¼ inches), length
176.3 cm (68½ inches)

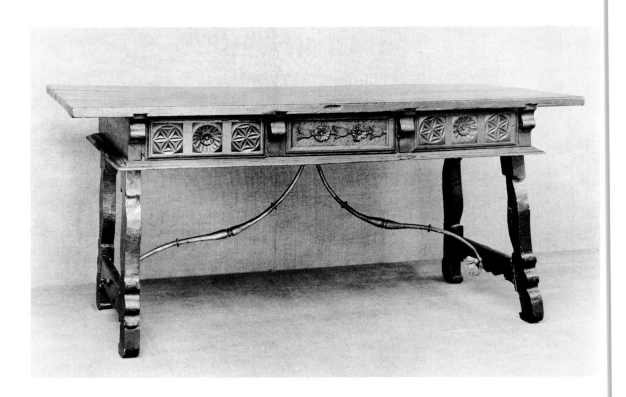

FIGURE 167 (S28)

TABLE (*back view*)
The back frieze is
separated into divisions
corresponding to the
drawer fronts

TABLE

S28

Below the overhanging top are three drawers separated by moulded blocks. The central drawer which has a moulded edge is divided by a stile, bearing the keyhole escutcheon, into two panels with gouged grounds. In each of these panels is carved in relief a small double rosette and a larger, eight-petaled rosette, to the centre of which a wooden knob pull is attached. The end drawers are divided into three square panels. The central panel displays an iron keyhole escutcheon against a quatrefoil. This square is flanked on either side by a panel carved with a double rosette centred in a wooden knob. Below the drawers is an outward-flared moulding. The back frieze is separated into divisions corresponding to the drawer fronts. The moulded, rectangular, central panel is ornamented with two rosettes flanked by connecting husks carved in high relief against a chipped ground. Each of the end panels contains three squares with rosettes or sexfoils. The table legs are slightly canted and suggest lyre-shaped supports. They are braced by simple, baluster irons.

FIGURE 168 (S29)

TABLE (*front view*)
XVII century. Walnut,
fitted with four drawers,
two of which pull out at
the centre and the other
two at the ends on the
opposite side. Height
84.5 cm (33$\frac{1}{4}$ inches),
width 80.5 cm (31$\frac{3}{4}$
inches), length 167.2 cm
(65$\frac{3}{4}$ inches)

FIGURE 169 (S29)

TABLE (*back view*)
Showing the two drawers
that pull out on the ends

TABLE

S29

The underframing of the table is fitted with four drawers, two of which pull out at the centre and the other two at the ends on the opposite side. They are separated by moulded brackets dovetailed to the underside of the plain, rectangular top. The faces of the two central drawers are divided into square panels linked at the base by a loop of the scroll which is carved upon them. To the centre of each is attached a wooden knob pull. The end panels are also divided into squares, each carved in relief with a rosette backed by crossed foliage. On the opposite side of the table, the central panels are each divided into two squares which are centred by circular double rosettes framed by four-way curved bands. The end drawers on this side are similar in design. To their centre rosettes, which are single and smaller, are fastened wooden knobs. Upon the division of one of the drawers is attached a keyhole escutcheon; the other is left blank, without a lock. Below the drawers is an outward-flared moulding. The supports of the table are lyre shaped and are grooved on the outer edge. Baluster irons brace them to the underframing of the table.

TABLE

S38

The side table has a plain top above an underframing fitted with three drawers, which display large rosettes boldly carved in high relief on leaves placed saltier-wise. The drawers have central drop pulls of iron attached beneath iron keyhole escutcheons. Two escutcheons, cut in the shape of *fleurs-de-lis*, show traces of red velvet backing, while the third, which is not original, is oval in shape and without velvet. Scrolled and fluted brackets, those at the ends topped with leaf capitals, separate the drawers. Below is an apron divided into three oblong panels, each carved in high relief with a central rosette flanked by curled leafage. The sides of the underframing are valanced. The straight legs and boxed stretchers are ring turned and blocked above ball feet.

CHAIR

S18

The heavy rectangular framework of the chair is ornamented by scorings and a central channel of gouge work carved along the surface of the straight front legs, their connecting valanced stretcher, and the front seat rail. Above the wooden seat with moulded edge an identical form of decoration is executed upon the round-ended and canted back posts, the top rail, valanced cross rail below, and their joining bar splats.

CHAIR

S67

Above the seat, the scored back posts terminate in slanting ends deeply cut with three parallel lines. Connecting the back posts are two rails joined by three upright bars which have jagged profiles. A zigzag line is incised across the centre of each scored rail and bar splat.

FIGURE 171 (S18)

CHAIR (*left*)
XVII century. Walnut; height of seat 41 cm (16¼ inches), total height 83.5 cm (32¾ inches)

FIGURE 172 (S67)

CHAIR (*right*)
XVII century. Walnut; height of seat 51.5 cm (20¼ inches), total height 90 cm (35½ inches)

FIGURE 173 (S68)

CHAIR (*left*)
XVII century. Walnut;
height of seat 49 cm (19¼
inches), total height 92 cm
(36¼ inches)

FIGURE 174 (S4)

CHAIR (*right*)
XVII century. Walnut;
paneled, with the open
back moulded and carved
in high relief with panels
and a central rosette.
Height of seat 53.5 cm
(21 inches), total height
97.5 cm (38½ inches)

FIGURE 175 (S19)

CHAIR (*left*)
XVII century. Walnut;
height of seat 44.5 cm
(17½ inches), total height
86.5 cm (34 inches)

FIGURE 176 (S20)

CHAIR (*right*)
XVII century. Walnut;
height of seat 44 cm (17¼
inches), total height
84.5 cm (33¼ inches)

CHAIR

S68

The arched top rail is attached to raked back posts with moulded ends. A vase-shaped splat connects this rail to a similar one below. The wooden seat is fastened by large nails to side rails in the form of corbels with moulded ends. The raked legs are joined at the sides by plain stretchers and at the front by a high, valanced stretcher.

CHAIR

S4

Raked and paneled posts with moulded ends frame the arcaded, open back. It is crested by a broken pediment which is moulded and carved in high relief with panels and a central rosette. Below the moulded-edged wooden seat, the front rail, shaped as an apron, is paneled, as are the faces of the front legs and their high, connecting, valanced stretcher.

CHAIR

S19

The solid, rectangular framework upholding the moulded, wooden seat has no decoration. Upon the surface of the back, made of canted uprights, rounded at the ends and connected by top and bottom rails, between which stand three, upright bar splats, is a pattern of sharply defined imbrications arranged in rows of three. A similar pattern is carved on a chair from the province of Santander at the Museum of Decorative Arts, Madrid.

CHAIR

S20

Petal-shaped imbrications are carved upon the faces of the canted and rounded back posts, the cross rails of the open back, the front legs, and the two, widely separated front stretchers. Two uprights which connect the cross rails of the back have petal-like contours. They are decorated with pairs of flaring chisel cuts. The broad, wooden seat is moulded at the front and sides.

FIGURE 177 (S65)

CHAIR (*left*)
XVII century. Walnut;
height of seat 48 cm (19
inches), total height
98 cm (38½ inches)

FIGURE 178 (S69)

CHAIR (*right*)
XVII century. Walnut;
height of seat 44.5 cm
(17½ inches), total height
83 cm (32¾ inches)

FIGURE 179 (S70)

CHAIR (*left*)
XVII century. Walnut;
height of seat 47 cm (18½
inches), total height
97 cm (38¼ inches)

FIGURE 180 (S71)

CHAIR (*right*)
XVII century. Walnut;
height of seat 47 cm (18½
inches), total height
87 cm (34¼ inches)

CHAIR

S65

Between the back posts, which are canted and surmounted by pointed finials, is a top rail rising at the crest in three arcs. This rail is connected by a central vase-shaped splat to a lower cross rail which has a scalloped edge. The legs are connected at the sides by moulded and valanced stretchers and by a scalloped stretcher at the front. The moulded-edged, wooden seat is supported upon seat rails resembling corbels.

CHAIR

S69

Canted back posts with moulded ends are connected by an arcaded, open back with four turned spindles standing on a valanced cross rail. The moulded seat is fastened by nails with large heads to side rails which are arranged as corbel supports with moulded ends. The legs are raked and joined at the front by a plain stretcher and at the sides by low, valanced stretchers.

CHAIR

S70

On the ends of the canted back posts, pear-shaped finials are carved. Between the posts is an arcaded top rail roughly moulded at the crest and along the arcade and decorated with two rosettes resembling pin wheels. This rail is joined by collared spindles to a crosspiece below, which is similarly shaped and moulded. The wooden seat with moulded edge, is fastened to the chair by nails.

CHAIR

S71

The rectangular framework of the chair is undecorated except for the valancing of the high, front stretcher and the turning of a row of spindles which stand between cross rails joined to the slightly raked back posts with rounded ends.

FIGURE 181 (S3)

BENCH

XVII century. Walnut, with a carved border of petal-shaped imbrications, surrounding a gilded metal plaque, nailed in a moulded panel, bearing the escutcheon of Pedro Alvarez de Acosta, bishop of Osma (1539–1563). Width 198 cm (6½ feet), depth 40.5 cm (16 inches), total height 90 cm (35½ inches)

BENCH

S3

The solid rectangular back is moulded and carved with a border of petal-shaped imbrications. Each section of the border is centred with a rosette from which the imbrications extend to the leaf-filled corners. A gilded metal plaque bearing the escutcheon of Pedro Alvarez de Acosta, bishop of Osma from 1539 to 1563, is nailed to a moulded panel in the centre of the back. As the bench is of seventeenth-century construction, the plaque was probably of earlier make. Lyre-shaped trestle supports carved at the front with three rows of gouging uphold the bench. The back legs continue above the seat to brace the back.

BENCH

S1

Conventionalized acanthus leafage is carved along the moulded top and sides of the rectangular back. The bottom edge is cut away in a series of six round arches. Below the top moulding appears a double row of acanthus leaves within a frame. Ovolo mouldings divide the back into twelve sections beneath this frame. The upper half of each division contains an imbricated moulding around two small rectangular-fielded panels edged with gouging. In the spandrels below, imbricated mouldings enclose a rosette carved in high relief. The back posts are raked and topped with leaf finials. They are joined by plain side stretchers to front legs turned and blocked above knobbed feet.

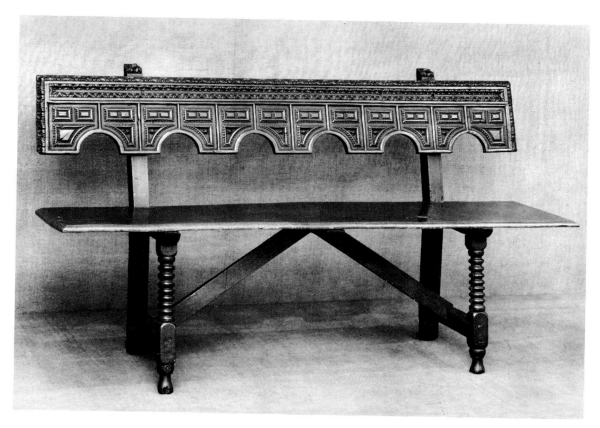

FIGURE 182 (S1)

BENCH (*reconstructed*) XVII century. The seat and back of this walnut bench do not belong together. Width 181 cm (71¼ inches), depth 43 cm (17 inches), total height 99 cm (38¾ inches)

FIGURE 183 (S2)

BENCH

XVII century. Chestnut; three medallions carved with flowers. Fluted bracket finials, and raked front legs scored and decorated with chisel cuts. Width 154 cm (60¾ inches), depth 35 cm (13¾ inches), total height 95 cm (37½ inches)

FIGURE 184 (S59)

CHEST

XVII century. Velvet-covered pine with mounts of brass and gilded iron. Such chests often stood upon low, heavily carved and gilded stands, or on feet. Height 48 cm (19 inches), width 106 cm (41½ inches), depth 52 cm (20¼ inches)

188

BENCH

S2

This small, chestnut bench has a solid, rectangular back upon which three medallions are carved. At the centre appears a two-handled vase filled with primly arranged flowers carved in high relief. At each side is a large rosette formed by a profusion of leaves and flowers carved around a central boss. Across the top of the back is a line of minute incised geometrical designs in the shape of crosses, dots, and circles. The faces of the raked front legs are scored and decorated with chisel cuts. The back posts, which terminate in fluted bracket finials, are also raked and connected to the front legs by plain side stretchers.

CHEST

S59

The rectangular chest, which has a slightly arched lid, rests upon a flat wooden base. Its worn and stained red velvet covering is not original. At the front are two large locks with single hasps. The brass lock plates are oval, pierced with borders of leaf scrolls. The gilded iron hasps are decorated below the hinge with a cusped valance from which a tassel is suspended. Pierced with circles, the hasps terminate in raised knobs. Angle braces of gilded iron cut with delicate S-scrolled leaf tracery reënforce the corners of the lid and the edges of the sides and base. The end plates to which carrying handles are attached are identical with the angle braces. The scrolled designs of the mountings are similar to those used by seventeenth-century ironsmiths of the School of Madrid. The interior of the chest is lined with cerise cloth. Pieces of the pink ribbons which supported the raised lid remain beneath brass-headed tacks. Chests of this type were often placed upon heavily carved and gilded stands or feet.

CHEST

S57

A single, straight-edged plank forms the base of the chest. The dove-tailing of the body is exposed. At the centre of the front is a large, iron lock plate crested with a *fleur-de-lis*. Both the plate and the long, slender hasp of the lock are painted red as are the carrying handles fastened to the sides. The slightly curved lid has a moulded, over-hanging edge with rounded cleats attached below each end. Three darts, painted red, are cut on the lid near the back, marking the approximate location of the ring hinges inside. At the front of the lid two large round-headed nails are hammered through to the upper part of the hasp. Within the chest at the right side near the top is constructed a narrow till with a flat lid. The lid is moulded along the front edge and incised with crossed darts and bands of parallel lines.

FIGURE 185 (S57)

CHEST

XVII century. Spanish cedar, with iron lock plate and handles painted red. Height 53.5 cm (21 inches), width 84.5 cm (33¼ inches), depth 48.5 cm (19 inches)

CABINET

S49

The lid of the cabinet, hinged at the bottom to fall forward, once was fastened by a large, iron hasp lock, only the inner plate of which now remains. The outer face of the lid shows an escutcheon. The arms quarterly are: I. *Argent, a bird gules*; II and III. *Sable, five roundels in saltier argent*; IV. *Argent, three bends gules*. Painted on the black interior of the lid is a green border and circular medallion filled with a large rosette. Green leaf scrolls appear in the corner segments of the design. The cabinet contains five drawers, of which two small ones are built into the bottom drawer. The deep mouldings around the three large drawers, the partitions between them, and the front edges of the sides of the chest are gilded. Each of the large drawers bears an inscription indicating its purpose. At the top is written LAP CORAL within a rectangular cartouche, on the middle drawer PVLVE in a cartouche at the left and CORDALES in a cartouche at the right, on the bottom drawer OMNES LAPIDES within a circular medallion. The top drawer probably contained coral, the second drawer, mortars for grinding stones to powders, and the third, uncut stones. Since powdered gems, especially coral, were used in medicines during this century, it is possible that the

FIGURE 186 (S49)

CABINET

XVII century. Walnut, painted and gilded. Top and base restored; three drawer pulls missing. Height 32 cm (12½ inches), width 28.5 cm (11¼ inches), depth 31 cm (12¼ inches)

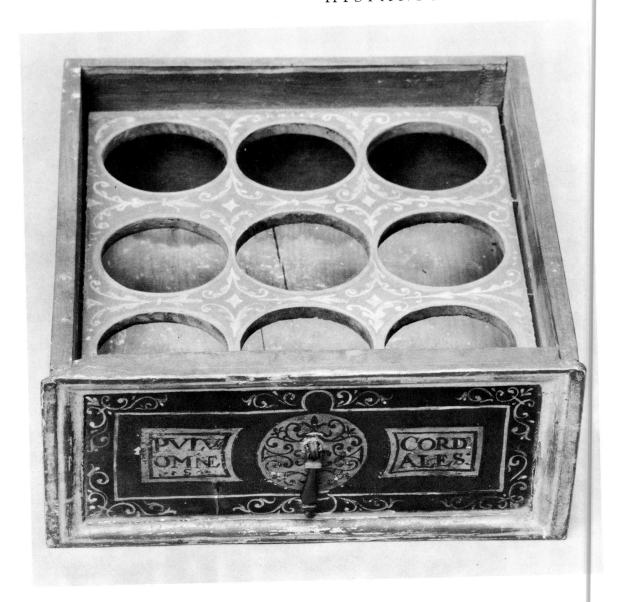

FIGURE 187 (S49)

CABINET (*interior of middle drawer*)

cabinet belonged to an apothecary. Drop pulls centre the drawers. The inside of the top drawer is scarlet as is that of the two small drawers below. A scarlet rack with nine round openings is fitted inside the middle drawer near the top. Within the bottom drawer is a hollow, rectangular centre surrounded by a wooden tier containing fourteen shallow, round wells. A gilded moulding frames the interior and central opening. Two narrow strips of wood attached near the top of this opening indicate that their original use was to support a cover. The framework around the wells and the inside of the hollow are painted robin's-egg blue. The wells are tinted with various colours.

192

BOX

S54

The flat top, sides, front, and back of the cedar box are veneered with parallel bands of yellow barberry and red-brown arbutus or briar chevrons pointing from a centre in opposite directions. The removal of the sliding lid discloses two deep inner compartments, the one at the back square and that at the front, rectangular. These compartments and the under side of the lid are lined with dark green velvet, probably dating from the late eighteenth or early nineteenth century. Below the compartments, at the front, is a small drawer also lined with green velvet. Its face, veneered with checkers, is edged with an applied, carved, zigzag moulding and is centred by a flat, round, wooden knob pull. The edges of the box above the drawer at the front, are banded with roping as are also the edges at the back and at the base of each side, where it appears above a narrow scalloped valance. The box is elevated slightly by round, flattened, and turned feet.

FIGURE 188 (S54)

BOX

XVII century. Cedar, veneered with barberry and briar or arbutus. Height 14 cm (5½ inches), width 9.6 cm (3¾ inches), depth 25 cm (9¼ inches)

BRAZIER

S79

FIGURE 189 (S79)

BRAZIER

Dated 1641. Walnut and brass foil. Height 72 cm (28¼ inches), diameter at top 80.5 cm (31¾ inches)

In the circular, scalloped top is a central aperture containing a flat, two-handled, brass pan with moulded edge. The top is upheld by four gilded and fluted, columnar legs which stand on a scalloped under shelf resting upon turned feet. The under shelf also contains a shallow, two-handled pan and, like the top, is covered with brass foil attached by rows of round-headed brass nails. On the scallops of both stories in *repoussé* appear the arms of Castilla, Castilla and León, Navarra, France, and of the Robles family. The Robles or Robres arms, *Argent, on a mount in base an oak tree proper supported by two goats rampant*, show a cross as a charge over the tree. An inscription around the top reads, ZARRAGOZA 1641 CONDE DE ROBLES.

FIGURE 190 (S79)

BRAZIER (*top view*)

CHOIR-STALLS

S62

There are three stalls with upper and lower ranges of seats. Above the upper range are figures of the Franciscans Louis of Brignoles, bishop of Toulouse, James of the Marches, and Daniel the Martyr. These figures with plump, smiling faces and habits carved with a few simple, deep folds, are in high relief against square panels separated by pilasters supported on brackets carved with cherubs' heads. The pilasters are decorated with nude half figures ending in husks. Above each saint is a cherub's head in a shell, and there are in the collection of the Hispanic Society three more which were above a doorway in the choir. The cresting is of leaf scrolls above the centre shell and of turned spires above the pilasters. Below the saints are narrow panels with leaf scrolls and with festoons of drapery supporting fruit. On panels at the backs of the upper range of seats are carved in low relief a mask between swags of fruit, a cartouche with the five wounds of Christ surrounded by leaf scrolls,

FIGURE 191 (S62)

CHOIR STALLS (LOWER RANGE)
Height 111.5 cm (44 inches), width 204 cm (6 feet, 8½ inches)

195

FIGURE 192 (S62)

CHOIR STALLS
(UPPER RANGE)

Late XVII century. Cedar
and mahogany, from the
Monastery of San
Francisco, Lima, Peru.
Height 300 cm (9 feet,
10 inches), width 217 cm
(7 feet, 1½ inches)

196

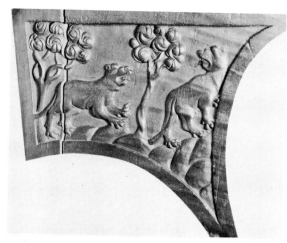

FIGURE 193 (S62)

CHOIR STALLS (*details*)

FIGURE 194 (S62)

CHOIR STALLS (*detail*)

and an urn with flowers flanked by addorsed birds. Edges of the arm supports are scrolled and carved with nude half figures terminating in husks and masks. Small panels at the sides contain, on the upper stalls, leaf scrolls and on the lower, leaf scrolls, fruit in a swag of drapery, a stag between trees, one beast pursued by another, and a vase with leaf scrolls. The misericords are carved with grotesque masks. Spaces below the seat, at back and sides, are patterned by panels with beveled edges. These stalls were once part of a choir of one hundred and thirty seats in a loft at the entrance of the Monastery of *San Francisco* in Lima, Peru. They were removed to allow space for an organ.

FIGURE 195 (S53)

INDO-PORTUGUESE
CABINET

XVII century. Redwood,
inlaid with ivory, ebony,
and mother-of-pearl.
Height 125 cm (49¼
inches), width 84.7 cm
(33¼ inches), depth
45.7 cm (18 inches)

CABINET

S53

The upper cabinet contains ten drawers built to look like twelve. This cabinet rests upon a receding chest of drawers which has legs carved to represent mermaids above square plinths set on ball feet. The base is separated from the top by a rounded moulding of ebony and is fitted with two upper drawers and a deep lower drawer. Delicate leaf scrolls of ebony inlaid upon a redwood ground cover the surface of the cabinet, except at the back. The faces of the drawers are decorated with foliated, ebony scrolls and are fitted with small knob pulls, each inlaid with a mother-of-pearl quatrefoil. Above the knobs are ivory keyhole escutcheons, oval in shape and surrounded by inlaid, ebony shields. Around the edges of the drawer fronts ebony mouldings are applied. Bandings of this wood, inlaid with ivory dots, separate the drawers and border the edges of the moulded top, front, and sides of the cabinet, as well as the top section of the base and the inlaid and moulded drawer fronts and side panels below. Bandings and mouldings are fastened by wooden pegs. A wider border of redwood, inlaid with ebony lozenges and ivory dots, surrounds the front and sides of the lower part of the base and divides the bottom drawer front vertically through the middle. The top of the cabinet is decorated with a central, rectangular panel framed by a convex moulding of ebony. This panel is inlaid with a circle containing a scrolled, mask-like design with eyes made of ivory and ebony circles. From each side of the circle springs a vase filled with leaf scrolls, the whole contained within an oval of ivory and ebony which fits inside the raised moulding. The corners of the rectangular panel display leaf scrolls. Outside the moulding, the top is inlaid with intricate leaf scrolls and four masks with ivory and ebony eyes. The patterns covering the sides of the cabinet are similar to those on the top. Across the forehead of each mermaid support, is set a row of ivory dots, and around each neck hangs a chain from which is suspended a pendant or amulet. The heads have smooth hair parted in the middle and rolled up at the ends. Each figure wears a leafy skirt with ivory-studded belt.

199

FIGURE 196 (S52)

INDO-PORTUGUESE
SMALL CABINET

XVII century. Mahogany,
inlaid with rosewood,
ebony, and ivory. Height
109 cm (43 inches), width
49.2 cm (19½ inches),
depth 37 cm (14½ inches)

CABINET

S52

The cabinet is divided into three stories. The top is fitted with six drawers, the middle with two, and the base with one large drawer. Around the top of the middle story runs a moulding. The legs of the cabinet, carved as mermaids, rest upon rectangular plinths moulded at top and base. The figures of these carved mermaid supports are highly conventionalized. Each drawer front has a pierced and scrolled brass keyhole escutcheon and two drop pulls backed by circular plates pierced with simple geometric star patterns. The upper corners of the top story and of the base above the heads of the mermaids are reënforced with pierced, brass angle braces. Mahogany, inlaid with an ogival inter-lacery of rosewood, ebony, and ivory, covers the front, sides, and top of the cabinet. The pattern is made up of linked quatrefoils outlined in rosewood and set with pieces of ebony centred with ivory dots. The drawer fronts, top and sides of the cabinet are banded with strips of veneer inlaid with rosewood. In the centre of the top and of each side of the upper story and base is a rectangular panel formed by strips of inlaid banding. Plain bandings separate the drawers.

FIGURE 197 (S52)

CABINET DRAWER
(*detail of inlay*)

201

FIGURE 198 (S12)

CHAIR
Early XVIII century.
Beech, upholstered with
painted leather. Height of
seat 45.1 cm (17¾ inches),
total height 118.5 cm
(46½ inches)

202

CHAIR

S12

The tall, canted back of the chair is upholstered with painted leather, secured by double rows of nails with round brass heads. This leather, coppery in hue, is stamped with a basket-weave design over which green-leafed pansies, carnations, roses, dahlias, and harebells are painted in natural colours. S-scrolled arm posts, carved at the base with a leaf, support the narrow, sloping and scrolled arms. Each arm is carved where it joins the back with a leaf and, at the rolled-over end, with a leaf and pendent husks in high relief. Leather upholstery on the wide seat extends over the seat rail, where it is fastened by double rows of brass-headed nails. The leather is broken, disclosing a covering of eighteenth-century figured silk brocade. Slender legs shaped in an incipient form of the cabriole, with scrolled feet set upon pear-shaped plinths, are hipped to the seat.

TRUNK

S80

The overhanging top of the leather trunk is strapped with iron bands pierced at the edge with scallops and incised with flowers and leaves. These bands divide the top into six panels embroidered with three-petaled flowers. Front and side edges of the top display small panels embroidered with birds and flowers, while the face of the trunk shows flowers, birds, and a lion. The colour of the embroidery has faded to a uniform tan. The single-hasped central lock has a round plate pierced with scrolled flowers. Flanking the lock plate are men dressed in eighteenth-century costumes of open greatcoats, knee breeches, long waistcoats, sashes, loose collars, and three-cornered hats. Each has one hand on his hip and the other raised with a glass in the gesture of making a toast. Embroidery on the sides of the trunk is similar to that at the front. Handles are attached to each side. The back of the chest is plain except for a small grotesque engraved on one hinge.

FIGURE 199 (S80)

MINIATURE TRUNK
XVIII century.
Embroidered leather.
Was possibly designed as
a traveling case for
holding liquor bottles.
Height 29 cm (11½
inches), width 48 cm
(19 inches), depth 35 cm
(13¾ inches)

CHEST

S56

The rectangular, trunk-shaped chest with a high, domed lid is fitted with two drawers in the base at the front. Corners of the body and lid are reënforced by angle braces of *fleur-de-lis* pattern. The outer hinges of the lid are of the same design. At the sides are carrying handles of twisted iron. The central lock of the chest has a long hasp with *fleur-de-lis* hinge and flat, notched tongue. Its lock plate, broken at the top, is pierced at crest and base. In the centre of each drawer is a roped and pierced, circular keyhole escutcheon. The chest is black painted with red, yellow, and green designs, now faded. Around the edges of the body and lid and across the front of the lid runs a border of flowers with four petals joined by scrolled leaves. Across the back of the lid is a wider border consisting of three large rosettes separated by scrolled leaves. Within the borders on top, front, back, and sides are fields diapered with interlaced quatrefoils.

FIGURE 200 (S56)

MEXICAN CHEST
XVIII century. Cedar; black, painted with red, yellow, and green designs. Height 48 cm (19 inches), width 64.5 cm (25½ inches), depth 33.5 cm (13¼ inches)

FIGURE 201 (S22)

MEXICAN CHAIR (*left*)
XVIII century. Mahogany,
upholstered in leather.
Height of seat 51.5 cm
(20¼ inches), total height
126.5 cm (49¾ inches)

FIGURE 202 (S21)

MEXICAN CHAIR
(*right*)
XVIII century. Poplar,
upholstered in leather.
Height of seat 49 cm
(19½ inches), total height
126.5 cm (49¾ inches)

206

CHAIR

S22

The high, tapering back is upholstered in leather attached by nails with ornamental, gilded brass heads. Some of the nail heads are small and round while others are large and pierced in the shape of rosettes. The back cresting is carved with bold C-scrolls which rise to a central leaf *fleuron* caught with drapery. Below the scrolls, in the centre of the cresting, stands a lion rampant. From the tops of the raked back posts, festoons of leafage extend part way down the sides. The leather upholstery of the saddle seat is fastened by round-headed nails. The seat rails are moulded. At the front is an apron valanced with broad S-scrolls and a pendant of foliage. The cabriole front legs are hocked and shouldered with feathered, savage masks hung with tassels. Below the masks the legs are laced with ribbons and are finished with large claw and ball feet. Gouged and scored serpentine stretchers centring beneath the seat in a *fleuron*, brace the legs. Further support is given by a bar stretcher at the back.

CHAIR

S21

This chair, similar in design to S22, appears to have been carved by the hand of a less skilled artisan. Unlike S22 it has seat rails at either side, valanced with scrolls like those ornamenting the apron.

NOTES

(1) Tramoyeres Blasco, Luis. *Instituciones gremiales, su origen y organización en Valencia*. Valencia, 1889. p. 78–80.

(2) *Ibid.* p. 80.

(3) The names of a number of seventeenth-century *ebanistas* are listed in Gestoso y Pérez, José. *Ensayo de un diccionario de los artífices que florecieron en Sevilla desde el siglo XIII al XVIII inclusive*. Sevilla, 1899. v. 1. p. 157–160.

(4) Tramoyeres Blasco. p. 112, 295.

(5) *Ibid.* p. 352–355. Guilds provided help for poor members by distributions of wheat during hard times and of money on such days as the birthday of the patron saint, which was celebrated with great ceremony. Dowries were given to the daughters of the needy and assistance to widows and orphans. At the time of a member's death, aid for burial was forthcoming, the treasurer of the carpenters' guild at Valencia being authorized to spend up to forty *pesetas* for this, and there was provision for entombment within the guild chapel.

(6) Capmany y de Montpalau, Antonio de. *Memorias históricas sobre la marina, comercio y artes de la antigua ciudad de Barcelona*. Madrid, 1779. v. 1, pt. 3, p. 122; Tramoyeres Blasco. p. 78.

(7) *Ibid.* p. 291.

(8) Capmany. p. 122.

(9) Tramoyeres Blasco. p. 216.

(10) *Ibid.* p. 220.

(11) *Ibid.* p. 224–225.

(12) Janer, Florencio. *Arcones tallados que se conservan en el Museo arqueológico nacional.* In *Museo español de antigüedades*. Madrid, 1877. v. 8, p. [239]–257. An idea of the costliness of the presents received by a high-born fifteenth-century lady from her bridegroom may be gained from the list of gifts from Don Rodrigo Ponce de León to Doña Beatriz Pacheco. Among the items are necklaces, bracelets, rings, and a girdle encrusted with gems and containing approximately twelve marks' weight of gold, two hundred oriental pearls, a saddle plated with silver, another made of silk, skirts of brocade, silk, and wool, gowns of the same, one edged with marten and one with ermine, dress materials, and headgear (*Ibid.* p. 250–251).

(13) Betí, Manuel. *Un inventari del Castell de Penyíscola, any 1451.* In *Estudis universitaris catalans.* January-December 1914. v. 8, p. [92]–102.

(14) González Hurtebise, Eduardo. *Inventario de los bienes muebles de Alfonso V de Aragón como infante y como rey (1412-1424).* In Institut d'estudis catalans. *Anuari.* 1907. v. 1, p. 178–179.

(15) Bofarull y Sans, Francisco de. *Alfonso V de Aragón en Nápoles.* In *Homenaje á Menéndez y Pelayo.* Madrid, 1899. v. 1, p. 629.

(16) Soler y Palet, Joseph. *L'art a la casa al segle XV.* In R. Academia de buenas letras de Barcelona. *Boletín.* January–March 1916. año 16, p. 289–305.

(17) Sanchis y Sivera, José. *Indumentaria y menaje doméstico en el siglo XV.* In *Las Provincias. Almanaque para 1935.* Valencia [1935]. año 55, p. 385–390. Another interesting fifteenth-century inventory appears in Aguiló, Estanislao K. *Inventari dels bens y heretat den Miquel Abeyar, notari, notable bibliofil mallorquí del siglo XV.* In Sociedad arqueológica luliana. *Boletín.* October 1898. año 14, p. 417–422; December 1898. año 14, p. 448–452.

(18) *Inventario del moviliario, alhajes, ropas, armería y otros efectos del Excelentísimo Señor D. Beltrán de la Cueva, tercer duque de Alburquerque. A°. 1560.* In *Revista de archivos, bibliotecas y museos.* January 31st, 1883. año 9, p. 19–37.

(19) Pérez Bueno, Luis. *El mueble.* Barcelona [1930]. p. [57?]. (*El tesoro artístico de España*)

(20) *Inventario del moviliario.* p. 32.

(21) Sempere y Guarinos, Juan. *Historia del luxo, y de las leyes suntuarias de España.* Madrid, 1788. v. 2, p. 80, 99–101.

(22) Bertrand, Louis. *Philippe II—Un ténebreuse affaire.* Paris [° 1929]. p. 54–55.

(23) *Inventario del moviliario.* p. 19–37.

(24) Williams, Leonard. *The arts and crafts of older Spain.* Chicago, 1908. v. 2, p. 38–46.

(25) Doménech, Rafael *and* Pérez Bueno, Luis. *Muebles antiguos españoles.* Barcelona [19–?]. p. xiii.

(26) Asúa y Campos, Miguel de. *El mueble en la historia.* Madrid [° 1930]. p. 132.

(27) Stirling-Maxwell, *Sir* William. *The cloister life of the emperor Charles V.* London, 1891. p. 484.

(28) Asúa y Campos. p. 138–139.

(29) *Inventario del moviliario.* p. 27.

(30) Byne, Arthur *and* Stapley, Mildred. *Spanish interiors and furniture.* New York [1922]. v. 1, p. vii.

(31) A nearly identical chest is in the collection of the Marchioness of Bermilla del Rey, Madrid. It stands on flattened ball feet on an inlaid table. Both chests have the customary flared plinths and overhanging lids.

(32) Schottmueller, Frida. *Furniture and interior decoration of the Italian renaissance.* New York, 1921. p. xviii; Odom, W. M. *A history of Italian furniture from the fourteenth to the early nineteenth centuries.* New York, 1918. v. 1, p. 94.

(33) Victoria and Albert museum, *South Kensington. Classified and descriptive catalogue of the art objects of Spanish production in the South Kensington museum, with an introduction by Señor Juan F. Riaño*. London, 1872. p. 5.

(34) Davillier, Jean Charles, *baron. Les arts décoratifs en Espagne au moyen âge et à la renaissance*. Paris, 1879. p. 71.

(35) Miquel y Badía, Francisco. *Muebles y tapices*. Barcelona, 1879. p. 80. (His *La habitación*. v. 2)

(36) R. Academia española, *Madrid. Diccionario de la lengua castellana*. Madrid, 1914. v. 1, p. 132.

(37) Doménech *and* Pérez Bueno. p. vii.

(38) Madoz, Pascual. *Diccionario geográfico-estadístico-histórico de España*. Madrid, 1846. v. 4, p. 25.

(39) Joaquín Enríquez speaks of curious examples of applied wood (usually box) over cloth, as being carved in Aragón, because of the great quantity that abounds in this old kingdom. Sociedad española de amigos del arte, *Madrid. Catálogo de la exposición de mobiliario español de los siglos XV, XVI y primera mitad del XVII*. [Madrid, 1918] p. 4.

(40) Almenas, *conde de las. Important medieval and early renaissance works of art from Spain*. New York, 1927. p. 133.

(41) *Ibid*. p. 256.

(42) Ruiz de Arcaute, Agustín. *Juan de Herrera, arquitecto de Felipe II*. Madrid, 1936. p. 188.

(43) [Ramis de Ayreflor y Sureda, José] *Familias extinguidas de Mallorca, IV: Berard*. In Societat arqueológica luliana. *Bolletí*. August–September 1919. any 35, p. 311–327.

(44) Sempere y Guarinos. v. 2, p. 99–101.

(45) Two interesting seventeenth-century inventories are to be found in Borja de San Román y Fernández, Francisco de. *El Greco en Toledo*. Madrid, 1910. p. 189-191, and Taboada Roca, Antonio. *Cotos y jurisdicciones de Galicia—Villar de Ferreiro.—El pazo.—Sus poseedores.—Inventarios de la casa en el siglo XVII*. La Coruña [1929].

(46) Vega Carpio, Lope Félix de. *La gatomaquia*. Madrid, 1807. p. 55; Calderón de la Barca, Pedro. *Comedias*. Madrid, 1761. v. 5, p. 154.

(47) Zayas y Sotomayor, María de. *Novelas amorosas y exemplares*. Zaragoça, 1637. p. [3] of Introduction, *tr*.

(48) Castillo Solórzano, Alonso de. *Tiempo de regozijo y carnestolendas de Madrid*. Madrid, 1627. *v°f* A3–*f* A4.

(49) Fernández Navarrete, Pedro. *Conservacion de monarquias y discursos politicos*. Madrid, 1626. p. 243–246.

(50) *Ibid*. p. 245–246, *tr*.

(51) Zabaleta, Juan de. *El dia de fiesta* pt. 2. *por la tarde*. Madrid, 1660. *f* 33–34.

(52) Carvajal y Saavedra, Mariana de. *Navidades de Madrid y noches entretenidas en ocho novelas*. Madrid, 1663. *f* 26–*v°f* 26.

(53) Byne, Arthur, *and* Stapley, Mildred. *Spanish interiors and furniture*. New York [1922]. v. 1, p. vi.

(54) Almenas. p. 248.

(55) Asúa y Campos. p. 158–159.

(56) *Ibid*. p. 160.

(57) Moreno Villa, José *and* Sánchez Cantón, Francisco Javier, *ed.* *Noventa y siete retratos de la familia de Felipe III por Bartolomé González*. In *Archivo español de arte y arqueología*. May–August 1937. p. 130–131, 143.

(58) Monreal, Julio. *Cuadros viejos*. Madrid, 1878. p. 295, *tr*.

(59) Calderón de la Barca, Pedro. *Comedias*. Madrid, 1763. v. 9, p. 445.

(60) Eberlein, Harold Donaldson *and* Ramsdell, Roger Wearne. *The practical book o Italian, Spanish, and Portuguese furniture*. Philadelphia, 1927. p. 247–248.

(61) Pearson, Joseph. *On the origin of spiral turning in furniture*. In *Apollo*. February 1939. v. 29, p. 66–69.

(62) Pérez Bueno. p. [59].

(63) Segovia (City). Ordinances, etc. *Tassa general y moderacion de precios de todos generos de mantenimientos y otras cosas*. Madrid, 1680. p. 29, 30, 39–40.

(64) Byne *and* Stapley. v. 1, p. vi.

(65) Breton de la Martinière, J. B. J. *L'Espagne et Portugal*. Paris, 1815. v. 5, p. 149.

(66) *Enciclopedia universal ilustrada*. Barcelona, J. Espasa [1921?]. v. 7, p. 471.

(67) Byne *and* Stapley. v. 1, p. vii.

(68) Vega Carpio. *Obras, pub. por la Real Academia española*. Madrid, 1895. v. 5, p. 320.

(69) Jourdain, M. *Goan ebony furniture*. In *The Connoisseur*. April 1917. v. 47, p. 194–196.

(70) Boehn, Max von. *Modes and manners*. London [ᶜ 1935]. v. 3, p. 77–78.

(71) Victoria and Albert museum. *Classified and descriptive catalogue*. London, 1872. p. xii–xiii.

(72) Castillo Solórzano. *La garduña de Sevilla y ançvelo de las bolsas*. Barcelona, 1644. f 27.

(73) Lerma, Francisco Gómez de Sandoval y Rojas, *duque* de. *Descripcion, e inventario de las rentas, bienes, y hazienda del cardenal duque de Lerma* [dated Valladolid, May 27th, 1622] vᵒf 25–29.

(74) Acuña, Luis Alberto. *Ensayo sobre el florecimiento de la escultura religiosa en Santa Fé de Bogotá*. [Bogotá]. 1932.

(75) Taboada Roca. p. 6.

(76) Byne *and* Stapley. v. 1, p. viii.

(77) Segovia (City). Ordinances, etc. *Tassa general*. p. 35–36, 39–40.

(78) Sempere y Guarinos. v. 2, p. 99–101.

(79) Caravajal y Saavedra. p. 4–5.

(80) Gardner, J. Starkie. *Charles II silver at Welbeck*. In *The Burlington magazine*. 1905. v. 7, p. 32–40, 103–111.

(81) Segovia (City). *Ordinances, etc. Tassa general*. p. 39–40.

(82) Breton de la Martinière. v. 5, p. 138.

(83) Bretón de los Herreros, Manuel. *Obras*. Madrid, 1884. v. 5, p. 185, *tr.*

(84) Kany, Charles E. *Life and manners in Madrid, 1750–1800*. Berkeley, Calif., 1932. p. 154.

(85) Breton de la Martinière. p. 139–142.

(86) Tenison, *Lady* Louisa Mary Anne (Anson). *Castile and Andalucía*. London, 1853. p. 399.

(87) Bretón de los Herreros. p. 186, *tr.*

(88) Tenison. p. 401.

(89) Carreras y Candi, Francisco, *ed. Folklore y costumbres de España*. Barcelona, 1931. v. 2, p. [513]–514.

(90) Townsend, Joseph. *A journey through Spain in the years 1786 and 1787*. London, 1791. v. 2, p. 114.

(91) Symonds, Ralph W. *Giles Grendley (1693–1780) and the export trade of English furniture to Spain*. In *Apollo*. December 1935. v. 22, p. 341–342; *English eighteenth century furniture exports to Spain and Portugal*. In *The Burlington magazine*. February 1941. v. 78, p. 57–60.

(92) Asúa y Campos. p. 243.

(93) *Ibid*. p. 243–244.

(94) An alcove bed typical of this century is illustrated in *Els mobles* by Joaquim Folch i Torres (*Vell i nou*. May 15th, 1915. any 1, p. 10).

(95) Dalrymple, William. *Travels through Spain and Portugal in 1774*. London, 1777. p. 14–15.

(96) Townsend. v. 2, p. 155.

(97) *Ibid*. p. 34.

(98) *Ibid*. p. 412.

(99) *Ibid*. p. 67, 70, 92, 265.

(100) Zabala y Lera, Pío. *España bajo los Borbones*. Barcelona, Buenos Aires [c 1930]. p. 155–157. (Colección Labor)

(101) Spanish luggage from the fifteenth through the nineteenth century, including boxes of this type, is described and illustrated by Julio Cavestany (*De los viajes retrospectivos. I. El equipaje*. In Sociedad española de excursiones. *Boletín*. June 1930. año 38, p. [131]–142, with 10 plates).

(102) Kany. p. 176–177.

(103) Mercer, Henry Chapman. *Ancient carpenters' tools*. Doylestown, Pa., 1929. p. 219.

(104) Townsend. v. 3, p. 178.

(105) *Ibid.* v. 1, p. 139.

(106) *Ibid.* v. 1, p. 116, 117.

(107) Uña y Sarthou, Juan. *Las asociaciones obreras en España (notas para su historia)*. Madrid, 1900. p. [277].

(108) Barrio Lorenzot, Juan Francisco del. *El trabajo en México durante la época colonial. Ordenanzas de gremios de la Nueva España*. México, 1920. p. 80–85.

(109) *Ibid.* p. 86–87.

(110) Terreros y Vinent, Manuel Romero de, *marqués de San Francisco. Las artes industriales en la Nueva España*. México, 1923. p. 125–127.

(111) Lamb, G. N. *The mahogany book*. Chicago [19–?] p. 4, 11.

(112) Cobo, Bernabé. *Historia del Nuevo mundo*. Sevilla, 1891. v. 2, p. 114–115.

(113) A document at the Hispanic Society, attributing the construction of the stalls in 1622 to Pedro Montes, a lay brother of the monastery, probably refers to an earlier set of stalls. Wethey, Harold Edwin. *Colonial architecture and sculpture in Peru*. Cambridge, Mass., 1949. p. 190–193; Gento Sanz, Benjamin. *San Francisco de Lima*. Lima, 1945. p. 189–192.

(114) Cobo. *Relaciones geográficas de Indias*. Madrid, 1881. v. 1, p. LVII–LVIII, *tr.*

(115) Patrón, Pablo. *Lima antigua*. Lima, 1935. p. 28–33; Gutiérrez de Medina, Cristóbal. *Viage de tierra y mar que hizo el señor Marqués de Villena*. Mexico, 1640. p. 34–35.

(116) Terreros. p. 131–135.

(117) Adaptation of Louis-the-Sixteenth style late in the eighteenth century is illustrated by furnishings of a drawing room in the Palace of Torre Tagle at Lima.

(118) Linschoten, Jan Huyghen van. *The voyage of John Huyghen van Linschoten to the East Indies, from the old English translation of 1598, ed. the first vol. by...Arthur Coke Burnell*. London, The Hakluyt society, 1885. v. 1, p. 193.

(119) Guimarães, Alfredo *and* Sardoeira, Albano. *Mobiliário artístico português*. Porto, 1934. p. 14.

(120) Lisboa. Museu das janelas verdes. *Mobiliário indo-português*. Lisboa, 1938.

(121) Danvers, Frederick Charles. *The Portuguese in India, being a history of the rise and decline of their eastern empire*. London, 1894. v. 1, p. 54.

(122) *Ibid.* v. 1, p. 315.

(123) Johnston, *Sir* Harry H. *Pioneers in India*. London, 1913. p. 135.

(124) Codrington, Kenneth de B. *Mughal marquetry*. In *The Burlington magazine*. February 1931. v. 58, p. 79–85.

(125) Birdwood, G. C. M. *The industrial arts of India*. London [1880]. p. 207.

(126) Edwards, Ralph *and* Codrington, Kenneth de B. *The Indian period of European furniture—II*. In *Apollo*. March 1935. v. 21, p. 130-134.

(127) Lisboa. Exposição retrospectiva de arte ornamental portugueza e hespanhola. *Catalogo illustrado*. Lisboa, 1882. v. 1, p. 236; v. 2, no. 173.

(128) Lisboa. Museu das janelas verdes. *Algumas obras de arte*. Lisboa, 1937.

REFERENCES

AGUIRRE, Victoria. *Colecciones de arte.* Buenos Aires [1927].

ALMENAS, José María de Palacio y Abarzuza, *conde de las. Important medieval and early renaissance works of art from Spain.* New York, 1927.

ASÚA Y CAMPOS, Miguel de. *El mueble en la historia.* Madrid [ᶜ 1930].

BARRIO LORENZOT, Francisco del. *El trabajo en México durante la época colonial. Ordenanzas de gremios de la Nueva España.* México, 1920.

BATLLE, Esteve. *El castell de Perelada i el seu mobiliari.* In *Vell i nou.* February 1921. època 2, v. 1, p. 379-383.

BETÍ, Manuel. *Un inventari del Castell de Penyíscola, any 1451.* In *Estudis universitaris catalans.* January–December 1914. v. 8, p. [92]-102.

BEVAN, Bernard. *Woodwork.* In *Spanish art.* London, New York, 1927. p. 87-97. (Burlington magazine monograph 2)

BOEHN, Max von. *Modes and manners, tr. by Joan Joshua.* London [ᶜ 1935]. v. 3-4.

BOFARULL Y DE SARTORIO, Manuel de. *Gremios y cofradías de la antigua corona de Aragón.* Barcelona, 1876–1910. v. 1, p. 318-330, 353-366; v. 2, p. 88-99. (Colección de documentos inéditos del archivo general de la corona de Aragón. v. 40-41)

BRANSCOMBE, Henry. *English styles in later Spanish woodwork.* In *International studio.* January 1928. p. 51-54.

BURLINGTON FINE ARTS CLUB. *Catalogue of an exhibition of Spanish art.* London, 1928.

BYNE, Arthur. *Old Spanish furniture.* In *Good furniture.* March 1915. p. 339-342.

BYNE, Arthur *and* STAPLEY, Mildred. *Spanish interiors and furniture.* New York [1922-25]. 3 v.

CAMACHO, Fabio. *Aspectos de Lima* [Lima, 1937?]

CAPMANY, Aurelio. *Lo que queda de los antiguos gremios barceloneses. V. Carpinteros.* In *Barcelona atracción.* June 1933. año 23, p. 190-193.

CAPMANY Y DE MONTPALAU, Antonio de. *Memorias históricas sobre la marina, comercio y artes de la antigua ciudad de Barcelona.* Madrid, 1779. v. 1.

CATALINA, Mariano. *Arcones ojivales del Museo arqueológico nacional y del renacimiento.* In *Museo español de antigüedades.* Madrid, 1876. v. 7, p. [535]-538.

CAVESTANY, Julio. *De los viajes retrospectivos. I. El equipaje.* In Sociedad española de excursiones. *Boletín.* June 1930. año 38, p. [131]–142.

CHANG, T'ien-Tsê. *Sino-Portuguese trade from 1514 to 1644.* Leyden, 1934.

CHILD, Theodore. *The Escurial.* In *Harper's new monthly magazine.* March 1893. v. 86, p. [531]–545.

COBO, Bernabé. *Fundación de Lima.* In *Relaciones geográficas de Indias.* Madrid, 1881. v. 1, p. IV–CXXXVI.

———— *Historia del Nuevo Mundo.* Sevilla, 1891. v. 2.

CODRINGTON, Kenneth de Burgh. *Mughal marquetry.* In *The Burlington magazine.* February 1931. v. 58, p. 79–85.

COLLIN, Bertha M. *The development of Portuguese furniture.* In *International studio.* July 1930. v. 96, p. 39–43.

———— *Portugiesische betten des 17. und 18. jahrunderts.* In *Pantheon.* September 1931. v. 8, p. 390–393.

CRENSHAW, Mary Mayo. *Some Peruvian furniture.* In *Antiques.* October 1928. v. 14, p. 313–318.

DAVILLIER, Jean Charles, *baron. Les arts décoratifs en Espagne au moyen âge et à la renaissance.* Paris, 1879. p. [69]–77.

DOMÉNECH, Rafael *and* PÉREZ BUENO, Luis. *Muebles antiguos españoles.* Barcelona [19–?].

EBERLEIN, Harold Donaldson. *The furniture of Latin colonial America.* In *Good furniture.* December, 1917. v. 9, p. 383–392.

———— *Old Spanish furniture.* In *Good furniture.* January 1917. p. 41–50, February 1917. p. 77–[85].

———— *Portuguese influence in European furniture.* In *Good furniture.* 1917. v. 9, p. 103–111.

———— *Spanish interiors—furniture and details from the 14th to the 17th century.* New York [1925].

———— *Spanish seating furniture of the eighteenth century.* In *Good furniture.* 1917. v. 9, p. 28–34.

———— *Spanish wall furniture of the eighteenth century.* In *Good furniture.* 1917. v. 9, p. 327–336.

———— *and* RAMSDELL, Roger Wearne. *The practical book of Italian, Spanish, and Portuguese furniture.* Philadelphia, 1927.

EDMUNDO, Luiz. *Rio in the time of the viceroys . . . tr. by Dorothea H. Momsen.* [Rio de Janeiro] 1936.

EDWARDS, Ralph *and* CODRINGTON, Kenneth de Burgh. *The Indian period of European furniture.—II.* In *Apollo.* 1935. v. 21, p. 130–134, 187–192.

REFERENCES

——— *The Indian period of European furniture. A reply to Dr. Slomann.* In *The Burlington magazine.* 1934. v. 65, p. 273–278.

——— *India and the west.* In *Apollo.* 1937. v. 26, p. 267–270.

——— *Letters. The Indian period of European furniture.* In *The Burlington magazine.* 1935. v. 66, p. 94.

ENRÍQUEZ, María Dolores. *El mueble español en los siglos XV, XVI, y XVII. Museo de artes decorativas.* Madrid [195?].

ESCRIVÁ DE ROMANÍ, José María, *marqués de Monistrol. Arcón ojival del siglo XV.* In *Museo español de antigüedades.* Madrid, 1873. v. 2, p. [273]–283.

ESTRADA, Genaro. *El arte mexicano en España.* México, 1937. p. 36–42. (Enciclopedia ilustrada mexicana 5)

FABRÉ Y OLIVER, J. *Muebles españoles del siglo XVI.* In *Vell i nou.* September 1921. època 2, v. 2, p. 187–193.

FERRÁN SALVADOR, Vicente. *Capillas y casas gremiales de Valencia.* Valencia, 1922–26.

FOLCH I TORRES, Joaquim. *Els mobles.* In *Vell i nou.* May 15th, 1915. any I, p. 9–12.

GARDNER, J. Starkie. *Charles II silver at Welbeck.* In *The Burlington magazine.* 1905. v 7, p. 32–40, 103–111.

GENTO SANZ, Benjamín. *San Francisco de Lima.* Lima, 1945.

GESTOSO Y PÉREZ, José. *Ensayo de un diccionario de los artífices que florecieron en Sevilla desde el siglo XIII al XVIII inclusive.* Sevilla, 1899. v. I.

GIMENO MICHAVILA, Vicente. *Los antiguos gremios de Castellón.* Castellón, 1933. p. 88–92.

GINER DE LOS RÍOS, Hermenegildo. *Artes industriales.* Barcelona [1905]. p. [77]–93.

GUERRA DUVAL, F. *Album das cvriosidades artísticas da Bahia.* Rio de Janeiro, 1928.

GUIMARÃES, Alfredo. *Mobiliario de Paço ducal de Vila Viçosa.* Lisboa, 1949.

GUIMARÃES, Alfredo *and* SARDOEIRA, Albano. *Mobiliário artístico português* (*elementos para a sua história*). Porto, 1924.

THE HISPANIC SOCIETY OF AMERICA. *Choir-stalls from the Monastery of San Francisco, Lima, Peru.* New York, 1928.

HUNTER, George Leland. *Veneering: the ancient art of marquetry.* In *Good furniture magazine.* 1926. v. 27, p. 274–279.

JANER, Florencio. *Arcones tallados que se conservan en el Museo arqueológico nacional.* In *Museo español de antigüedades.* Madrid, 1877. v. 8, p. [239]–257.

JOURDAIN, M. *Goan ebony furniture.* In *The Connoisseur.* 1917. v. 47, p. 194–196.

KANY, Charles Emil. *Life and manners in Madrid, 1750–1800.* Berkeley, Calif., 1932.

LAMB, George Newton. *The mahogany book.* Chicago [19–?].

LÁZARO Y GALDIANO, José. *La colección Lázaro de Madrid.* Madrid, 1926–27. 2 v.

LEGUINA Y VIDAL, Enrique de, *barón de la Vega de Hoz. El arte en el hogar.* Madrid, 1918.

LOZOYA, Juan Contreras y López de Ayala, marqués de. *Muebles de estilo español.* Barcelona, 1962.

McNEIL, Paul A. *A Peruvian art collection in Washington.* In The Pan American union. *Bulletin.* 1936. v. 70, p. 639–650.

MARTÍNEZ FEDUCHI, Luis. *Antología de la silla española.* Madrid [1957].

———— *El Hospital de Afuera, Fundacion Tavera-Lerma.* Madrid [1950].

———— *Los Museos Arqueológico y Valencia de D. Juan.* Madrid [1950].

———— *Spanish furniture of the XVIIth and XVIIIth centuries.* In *Apollo.* January 1964, p. 35–39.

MÁRQUEZ DE LA PLATA Y ECHENIQUE, Fernando. *Los muebles en Chile durante los siglos XVI, XVII y XVIII.* Santiago de Chile, 1933.

MARTORELL, Jerónimo. *Interiores.* Barcelona, 1923. (Exposición de Barcelona)

MAYER, August Liebmann. *El mobiliario español.* In *Vell i nou.* May 1921. època 2, v. 2, p. 52–57.

MÉLIDA, José Ramón. *Escorial—II.* Barcelona [1915].

MERCER, Henry Chapman. *Ancient carpenters' tools.* Doylestown, Pa., 1929.

MIQUEL Y BADÍA, Francisco. *Muebles y tapices.* Barcelona, 1879. (His *La habitación.* v. 2)

———— *Historia del mueble.* Barcelona, 1897. p. [1]–184. (Historia general del arte. v. 8)

MUSEU NACIONAL DE ARTE ANTIGA (Lisboa). *Influéncias do Oriente na arte portuguesa continental, a arte nas provincias portuguesa do Ultramar.* 1957.

ODOM, William Macdougal. *A history of Italian furniture from the fourteenth to the early nineteenth centuries.* New York, 1918. v. 1.

ORDUÑA VIGUERA, Emilio. *La talla ornamental en madera.* Madrid [c 1930].

OTT, Horace Wesley. *Spanish furniture of the eighteenth century.* In *The Antiquarian.* November 1929. p. 43–45, 70.

PEARSON, Joseph. *On the origin of spiral turning in furniture.* In *Apollo.* 1939. v. 29, p. 66–69.

PÉREZ BUENO, Luis. *El mueble.* Barcelona [1930]. (El tesoro artístico de España)

PÉREZ-VALIENTE DE MOCTEZUMA, Antonio. *Evolución del mueble colonial en el Río de la Plata. La colección de Don Gustavo M. Barreto.* In *La Nación.* Buenos Aires, January 5th, 1930. p. 7–8. (rotogravure sección)

RIAÑO Y MONTERO, Juan Facundo. *The industrial arts in Spain.* London, 1890.

ROMERO DE TORRES, Enrique. *Catálogo monumental de España. Provincia de Cádiz (1908–1909).* [Madrid] 1934. 2 v.

SANCHIS Y SIVERA, José. *Indumentaria y menaje doméstico en el siglo XV.* In *Las Pro-*

REFERENCES

vincias. Almanaque para 1935. Valencia [1935]. año 55, p. 385-390.

SCHOTTMUELLER, Frida. *Furniture and interior decoration of the Italian renaissance.* New York, 1921.

SEGOVIA (City). *Ordinances, etc. Tassa general y moderacion de precios de todos generos de mantenimientos y otras cosas.* Madrid, 1680.

SHIPWAY, Verna and Warren. *Mexican interiors.* N. Y., 1962.

SLOMANN, Vilhelm. *The Indian period of European furniture.* In *The Burlington magazine.* 1934. v. 65, p. 113-126, 157-171, 201-214; 1935. v. 66, p. 21-26.

SMITH, Robert Chester. *Portuguese Chippendale chairs.* In *Antiques.* July 1962, v. 82, p. 54-7.

——— *Portuguese furniture in the seventeenth century.* In *The Connoisseur.* April 1959, v. 143, p. 194-197, May 1959, v. 143, p. 268-271.

——— *Portuguese Hepplewhite and Sheraton chairs.* In *Antiques.* August, 1962. v. 82, p. 168-71.

SOCIEDAD ESPAÑOLA DE AMIGOS DEL ARTE, *Madrid. Aportación al estudio de la cultura española en las Indias; catálogo general ilustrado.* [Madrid, 1930]

——— *Catálogo de la exposición de mobiliario español de los siglos XV, XVI y primera mitad del XVII.* [Madrid, 1918]

——— *Exposición del antiguo Madrid; catálogo general ilustrado.* Madrid [1926].

SOLÁ, Miguel. *Historia del arte hispano-americano.* Barcelona, Buenos Aires [c 1935]. (Colección labor)

SYMONDS, Ralph W. *Furniture from the Indies.* In *The Connoisseur.* 1934. v. 93, p. 283-289.

——— *Giles Grendey (1693-1780) and the export trade of English furniture to Spain.* In *Apollo.* 1935. v. 22, p. 337-342.

——— *English eighteenth century furniture exports to Spain and Portugal.* In *The Burlington magazine.* February 1941. v. 78, p. 57-60.

TAULLARD, Alfredo. *El mueble colonial sudamericano.* Buenos Aires, 1944.

TERREROS Y VINENT, Manuel Romero de, *marqués de San Francisco. Las artes industriales en la Nueva España.* México, 1923.

THOMSON, Charles D. *Art history revealed. V. The unsuspected influence of the Spanish Moors.* In *Good furniture.* March 1917. p. 159-170.

TRAMOYERES BLASCO, Luis. *Instituciones gremiales, su origen y organización en Valencia.* Valencia, 1889.

WETHEY, Harold Edwin. *Colonial architecture and sculpture in Peru.* Cambridge, Mass.. 1949.

WILLIAMS, Leonard. *The arts and crafts of older Spain.* Chicago, 1908. v. 2, p. 1-86. (The world of art series)

ZIMMERN, Nathalie Herman. *A Peruvian bargueno, colonial variation of the European writing cabinets.* In *Gazette des Beaux-Arts.* March 1947, v. 31, p. 109-22.

INDEX

INDEX

THE PHOTOGRAPHS

The photographs included in this book are reproduced through the courtesy of the following sources (numbers given are figure numbers, not page numbers). American Museum of Natural History: 78 (*details*); D. Anderson, Rome: 10; Archivo de Arqueología Catalana; Barcelona: 1, 2, 3, 14, 31, 32, 73, 94; Archivo "Mas", Barcelona: 8, 15, 16, 17, 33, 34, 35, 49, 53, 97; Art Institute of Chicago: 99, 106; Art Association of Montreal: 21; Avilés Hermanos, Lima: 103; William E. Boggs, N. Y.: 48, 51; Brooklyn Museum: 78 (*front view*); Arthur Byne: 20, 55, 59, 60, 61, 62, 70, 76, 88, 91; Arthur Byne and Mildred Stapley, in *Spanish interiors and furniture*, N. Y. 1922: 39, 98; Lawrence X. Champeau, N. Y.: 25, 64; City Art Museum, St. Louis: 41; Cleveland Museum of Art, John Huntingdon Collection: 30; A. C. Cooper & Sons, London: 56; Don Eduardo Dibós Dammert: 78; Denver Art Museum: 42; Genaro Estrada, in *El arte mexicana en Espana*, Mexico, 1937: 107; José María Florit, in *Museum*, v. 7, 1932: 29; F. Guerra Duval, in *Album das curiosidades artisticas da Bahia*, Rio de Janeiro, 1928: 112, 113; Foto Gudiol, Barcelona: 74; Rudolf Himpsl, Munich: 40; Hispanic Society of America, N. Y.: Frontispiece, 9, 18, 19, 22, 43, 44, 52, 55, 65, 67, 68, 69, 70, 76, 77, 80, 81, 82, 84, 86, 87, 89, 100, 101 and 118 to 202; George E. Hutchinson, in *The clear mirror*, Cambridge (England), 1936: 116; Isabella Stewart Gardner Museum, Boston: 6, 50, 96; Jonals Co., Copenhagen: 114; M. Junghandel, in *Die Baukunst Spaniens*, Dresden 1900?: 18; Kunstgewerbe Museum, Cologne: 11, 37; Kunstgewerbe Museum, Dresden: 58; Kunstgewerbe Museum, Dusseldorf: 54; Willy Lang, Córdoba, Argentina: 110, 111; Metropolitan Museum of Art, N. Y.: 26, 95; Minneapolis Institute of Arts: 63; Museo Episcopal, Vich: 72, 75, 83; Museum Meermanno Westreenianum, The Hague: 115; *National Geographic Magazine*: 102; Österreichisches Museum für Angewandte Kunst, Vienna: 36; Philadelphia Museum of Art: Jacket (*front*), 90; N. Portugal, Madrid: 40; Rhode Island School of Design, Providence: 7, 71; Saez Món y Novás, Pontevedra: 45, 46; Museo Salzillo, Murcia: 93; Sensor Studios, San Diego: 27; F. Serra, Barcelona: 12, 92; Smithsonian Institution, Washington, D. C.: 108; Marie Sterner Galleries, N. Y.: 57; Vega Inclán Collection, Madrid: 28; J. Ruiz Vernacci, Madrid: 5, 66; Victoria and Albert Museum, London: 4, 23, 38, 79, 85, 117; Georg Weise, in *Spanische plastik aus sieben jahrhunderten*, Reutlingen, 1929: 13; and the M. H. de Young Memorial Museum, San Francisco: 24.

THE AUTHOR

GRACE HARDENDORFF BURR, a native of New England, studied Spanish at Simmons College, and in 1930 came to New York to join the staff of the Hispanic Society of America. Three years later she was appointed Curator of Furniture. She compiled a definitive catalogue of the furniture in the collection of the Hispanic Society, and earned recognition as an expert on the history of Spanish and Portuguese furniture. For many years she served on the editorial board of the Society, and her articles and translations have appeared in a number of publications. She left the Society in 1938 to move, with her husband, Alan Turner Burr, to a 200-year-old house in Massachusetts. In 1939 the Society honored her by electing her a Corresponding Member.

THE BOOK

The text of this book is set in monotype Caslon, a font modeled on the letters cut by the English type-founder William Caslon about 1722.

Born in 1692, Caslon was originally apprenticed to an engraver of gun-locks and barrels in London, and was not initiated as a letter-founder until he was about 28. His types, although used in books, did not appear on a specimen sheet until 14 years later, in 1734. The specimen sheet sealed his fame, and assured the success of the foundry that remained in the Caslon family for a century and a half.

Caslon modeled his letters after Dutch types, but his are more interesting and more delicate, and avoid the monotony of the Dutch faces. Sturdy and well-proportioned, comfortable rather than elegant, they represent the best of the English tradition in typography.

The captions are set in Garamond and the display type is Goudy Light.

INVENTORY 74.

INVENTORY 1983